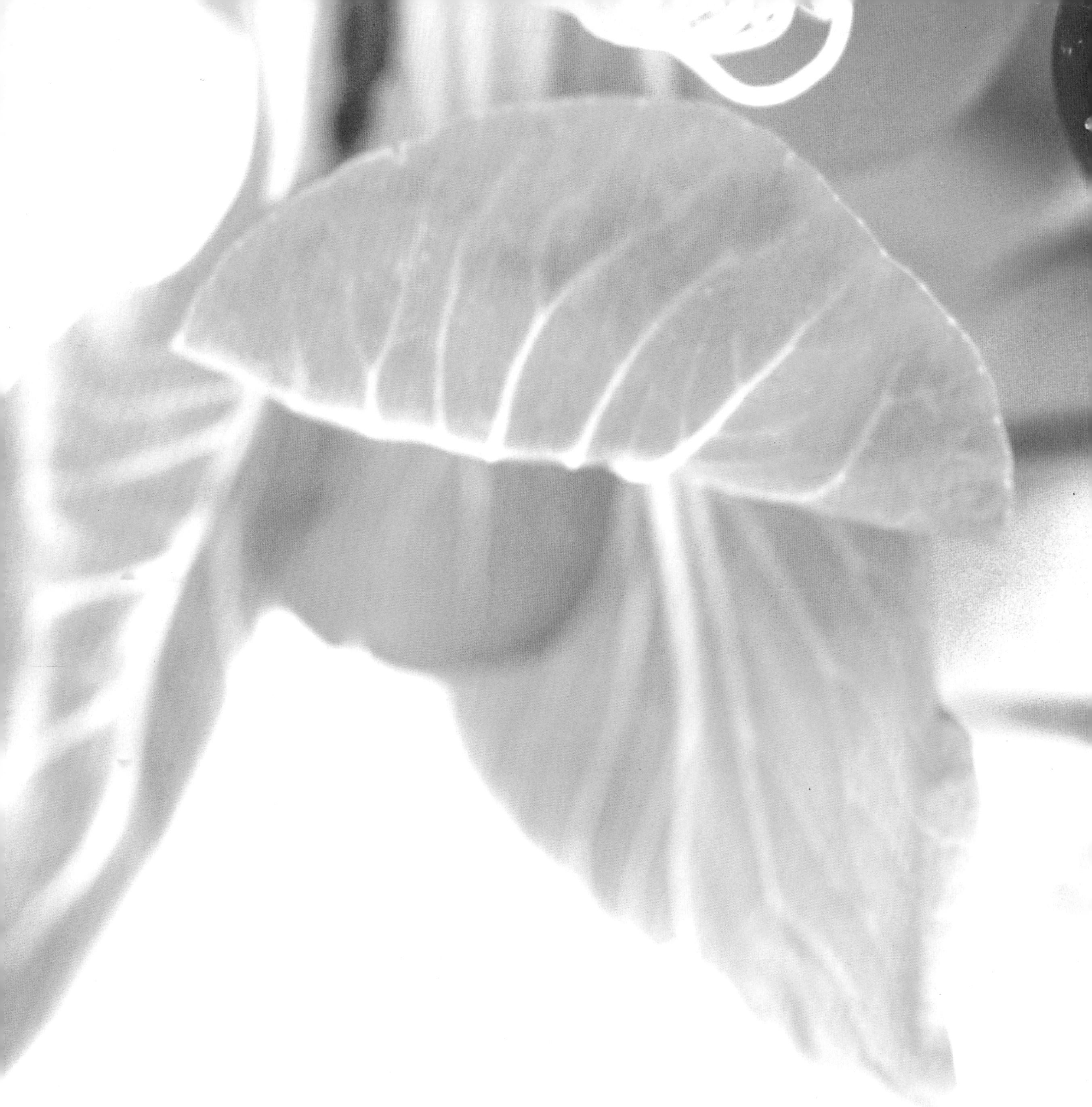

complete
chinese
cooking

complete
chinese
cooking

hamlyn

First published in the U.K. in 1997
by Hamlyn an imprint of Octopus Publishing Group Ltd
2–4 Heron Quays
London E14 4JP

Copyright © 1997, 2000 Octopus Publishing Group Ltd

This edition first published in 2000

ISBN 0 600 60191 9

Produced by Toppan
Printed in China

A CIP catalogue record for this book is available from the British
Library

NOTES
Both metric and imperial measurements have been given in all
recipes. Use one set of measurements only, and not a mixture of
both.

Standard level spoon measurements are used in all recipes.
1 tablespoon = one 15 ml spoon
1 teaspoon = one 5 ml spoon

Eggs should be medium to large unless otherwise stated.
The Department of Health advises that eggs should not be
consumed raw. This book contains dishes made with raw or
lightly cooked eggs. It is prudent for more vulnerable people such
as pregnant and nursing mothers, invalids, the elderly, babies and
young children to avoid uncooked or lightly cooked dishes made
with eggs. Once prepared, these dishes should be kept refrigerated
and used promptly.
Meat and poultry should be cooked thoroughly. To test if poultry
is cooked, pierce the flesh through the thickest part with a skewer
or fork — the juices should run clear, never pink or red. Do not
re-freeze poultry that has been frozen previously and thawed.
Do not re-freeze a cooked dish that has been frozen previously.

Milk should be full fat unless otherwise stated.

Nut and Nut Derivatives
This book includes dishes made with nuts and nut derivatives. It
is advisable for customers with known allergic reactions to nuts
and nut derivatives and those who may be potentially vulnerable
to these allergies, such as pregnant and nursing mothers, invalids,
the elderly, babies and children to avoid dishes made with nuts
and nut oils. It is also prudent to check the labels of pre-prepared
ingredients for the possible inclusion of nut derivatives.

Pepper should be freshly ground black pepper unless otherwise
stated.

Fresh herbs should be used, unless otherwise stated. If
unavailable, use dried herbs as an alternative, but halve the
quantities stated.

Measurements for canned food have been given as a standard
metric equivalent.

Ovens should be pre-heated to the specified temperature — if
using a fan-assisted oven, follow the manufacturer's instructions
for adjusting the time and the temperature.

Contents

Introduction

Chinese people are passionate about food. Chinese families spend hours gathered round the table, planning what they are going to eat, eating it, and then reminiscing about their favourite dishes and preferred cooking methods. But food is associated with much more than just delicious tastes and sustenance. Eating well is actually thought to be essential to living well.

When Chinese people meet each other, they say 'Chi fan le mei yo?' which means, literally, 'Haven't you eaten rice yet?' This is an everyday greeting, and is tantamount to saying 'How are you?' in English. It also entails a wish for a person's good health and happiness.

Four schools of Chinese cookery

In China, there are an estimated 55 ethnic minorities, each of which has contributed something different to the many and varied culinary skills to be found in this vast country. It is hardly surprising, then, that there is no single Chinese way of cooking. There are, rather, a great many culinary traditions.

These can be grouped into the four main schools of Chinese cookery which depend largely on the climate and, in turn, on the availability of local produce.

The four main schools of Chinese cuisine are:
- *Cantonese*   - *Huaiyang*   - *Szechuan*   - *Beijing*

Cantonese

Cantonese cooking is found mostly in the Kwangtung province of China, which is in the south of China near Hong Kong. Cantonese food is probably the best known in the West, because many Chinese families emigrated from this area of China to Europe and America in the nineteenth century.

Cantonese cooking tends to be regarded as the *haute cuisine* of China. This probably harks back to the brilliant chefs of the Imperial Court, who fled to Guangzhou, or Canton, when the Ming dynasty was overthrown in 1644.

The Cantonese are keen on exotic delicacies, such as snake, frog's legs and dog. Cantonese cooking also owes much to the ready availability of locally caught fish and shellfish. There are therefore a great many seafood specialities. For example, vegetables are often filled with a shellfish stuffing.

Another Cantonese speciality is its delicious sweet and sour recipes, and its dumplings, or *dim sum*, which are served as a light lunch or afternoon tea. The area has come to be known as one of the rice bowls of China and, not surprisingly, rice is the staple diet.

The Cantonese avoid heavy, overpowering flavours such as garlic and spices. They prefer, instead, to rely for their flavourings on the use of soy, hoisin and oyster sauces, all of which help achieve a subtle blend of aromas and colours. Food is often slightly undercooked, which allows the natural flavours, textures and colours to be preserved. Stir-frying and steaming are therefore the most popular cooking methods.

Huaiyang

Huaiyang cuisine is found mainly around Yangchow, on the eastern coast of China bordering on the East China Sea. The area has some of the most fertile land in China, and has a rich variety of fresh fruit and vegetables at its disposal. Not surprisingly, it is noted for its vegetarian cuisine. The area is dominated by the estuary of the Yangtze River, and the coastline is very long. Fresh fish and shellfish are therefore plentiful.

Specialities from this area include many steamed dishes, including the popular savoury dumplings. There are also many noodle dishes, renowned for their subtle flavours, which hail from the Yangtze River delta.

Other regions of eastern China include Nanking, which is famous for its succulent duck recipes, and Shanghai, which has a rather more sophisticated cuisine of its own. Cooks in the East of China are particularly keen on stir-frying, steaming, blanching and red-cooking (which means slow simmering in dark soy sauce). The food has acquired a reputation for richness, because of its widespread use of oil and sugar in savoury dishes.

Szechuan

This is the western region of China, which is entirely inland. Fruit and vegetables are easily available, as are pork, poultry and fish. Dishes that come from the Szechuan region tend to be richly flavoured, spicy, even hot. This is largely due to the fiery chilli peppers, hot pepper oil, and the Szechuan peppercorns, ginger, onions and garlic, all of which are widely used in the area.

Beijing

Beijing (formerly known as Peking in the West) is not only the capital city of China, but also its culinary centre, because chefs from all the different regions of the country have gravitated to Beijing over the centuries, bringing with them specialities from their own particular area. Its cuisine therefore tends to be very varied.

Best known of all, perhaps, is its glorious dish still known by its old name of Peking Duck. This consists of succulent pieces of crispy duck served in steamed mandarin pancakes with plum sauce, spring onions and cucumber. This is an elaborate banquet dish, which probably hails from the fact that the Imperial Court of China was based in the city. You will find the recipe for this superb dish on page 92.

This area is also famous for its sweet and sour dishes, which come from the northern province of Honan on the Hwang Ho River.

Beijing is in the north of China, where the climate can be harsh. Fresh vegetables are only available at certain times of the year, and people have therefore learned how to preserve foods to see them through the long, cold winters. Vegetables that store well, such as potatoes, turnips and cabbages, are widely used, and preserved ingredients such as dried mushrooms and pickled fruits and vegetables are also popular.

Flavours tend to be strong, owing to the widespread use of garlic, leeks, onions, sesame seeds and oil, and sweet bean sauce.

Grains other than rice tend to be used as the staple

ingredients. These include wheat, corn and millet, which the northerners eat in the form of bread, noodles, dumplings and pancakes.

Store cupboard ingredients

There are many ingredients that you will find in your store cupboard which will come in useful in Chinese cookery. Some of these are included below.

Rice

There are many different types of rice, including long-grain, short-grain and glutinous varieties. Brown rice is not used in China, where most people dislike its texture.

The most popular rice is long-grain white rice. Glutinous, or sticky, rice is a medium-grain rice which becomes sticky and sweet when boiled. It is widely used in baking and for dessert dishes. Despite its name, it is completely gluten-free!

Garlic

Chinese cookery relies on the use of garlic as an essential flavouring. Buy fresh garlic, which may be used whole, chopped or crushed, and keep it in a cool dry place. Garlic should not be kept too long in the refrigerator, it may go mouldy or begin sprouting.

Oils

Oil is commonly used as a cooking medium. Groundnut oil is pleasantly mild and is excellent for stir-frying and deep-frying. Safflower and sunflower oils are also good.

Sesame oil has a distinctive nutty taste and is often used in Chinese cookery. Do be warned however — it is more commonly used as a seasoning than as a cooking oil because it tends to burn easily. Sesame oil is often added at the last minute to add flavour and to finish a dish.

Specialist ingredients

Authentic Chinese cooking is not possible without the use of certain specialist ingredients which add a distinctive flavour and colour. Specialist Chinese ingredients are easily available from supermarkets and Chinese food stores. Because so many Chinese people live abroad, major cities have their own Chinatown area, with colourful shops, restaurants and food stores. Just browsing around these gives a fascinating glimpse into the rich diversity of the culture. Another excellent source of oriental ingredients is your nearest large supermarket. People have become so interested in Chinese food that a good range of basic ingredients is available there. You will find special features throughout this book which supply detailed information about specialist ingredients.

Preparing the ingredients

Chinese cookery places the emphasis on preparing the ingredients rather than cooking them. There is a lot of cutting, chopping, dicing and shredding involved, and this is the time-consuming part of the process as the cooking time is relatively short.

Cooking methods

Common methods of cookery including stir-frying, steaming, and red braising.

Stir-frying

This is the most common method of all, and entails simply frying foods in a small amount of oil over high heat, stirring constantly. This method ensures that the food is sealed and cooked very quickly, which allows it to maintain its flavour, texture and colour — all so important to the success of the finished dish. The key to this method involves having the ingredients ready before

you start cooking, which will take only minutes. Stir-fried foods must not be overcooked or greasy.

Steaming

This is a very healthy way of preparing food, and again allows foods to hold their original flavour, colour and texture. It is particularly well suited to foods that have a delicate taste or texture, such as fish and vegetables.

Red-braising

This method of cooking is peculiar to China. It entails stewing food in a mixture of soy sauce, water and sugar, with additional flavourings of root ginger, spring onion and rice wine. The food takes on a red tinge during the cooking process — hence the name. It is particularly well suited to tougher cuts of meat and certain vegetables that do not cook quickly.

Eating Chinese-style

The easy informality of Chinese eating makes meal times very relaxed and pleasurable. Rather than a set pattern of starter, main course and dessert, a selection of various dishes is set on the table. This does not mean that a

Chinese meal is set out at random — the selection of dishes will be carefully chosen to complement each other, in order to achieve the ideals of balance and harmony. Contrasts of taste, texture and colour are very important. Each guest has a bowl, chopsticks and perhaps a decorative porcelain spoon for soup and everyone helps themselves to the food.

One major advantage is that this means far less washing-up, as the same bowl can be used throughout the meal. If you wish to serve wine with your meal, try light fruity wines in both red or white varieties. If you prefer, you can serve tea — jasmine is extremely popular. A pretty oriental teapot is a nice touch, and these are easily available from Chinese stores.

Using a wok

A wok, with its specially rounded base and sloping sides, is the perfect piece of equipment for stir-frying. Its shape allows the heat to spread evenly over the surface which encourages rapid cooking, and its depth allows you to toss foods quickly without spilling them.

Choose a large wok with deep sides. The best ones are made of carbon steel rather than stainless steel or aluminium, which tend to scorch. There are also non-stick woks available on the market, but these are more expensive and cannot be seasoned (see below), which detracts from the flavour of the food that is cooked in them. To season a wok, scrub it first to remove the machine oil which is applied by the manufacturer to protect it in transit, and then dry it and put it on the hob over a low heat. Add 2 tablespoons of cooking oil, and rub this all over the surface using absorbent kitchen

paper. Heat the wok slowly for 10–15 minutes and then wipe with more paper. Repeat the coating, heating and wiping process until the kitchen paper comes away clean.

You should never need to scrub your wok again. Just wash in plain water and dry thoroughly by putting it over low heat for a few minutes before putting it away. This will prevent your wok from rusting.

Accessories you may find useful with your wok include:
• a stand, which is a metal ring designed to keep the wok steady on the hob and is essential if you want to use your wok for steaming, deep-frying or braising.
• a lid, which is dome-shaped and absolutely essential if you use your wok for steaming. You can, of course, use any other sort of lid which fits snugly over the top of the wok or, failing that, you can use aluminium foil.
• a bamboo brush, which is a bundle of stiff, split bamboo and is used for cleaning the wok without scrubbing it.

Fresh stock recipes

You will find it very useful to refer to these basic recipes as they are required throughout the book.

A good stock is easy and cheap to make, with only a few basic ingredients. It is not necessary to resort to stock cubes, when the flavour of a fresh aromatic broth is far superior. For beef or fish stock you should be able to find the bones you need at the butcher or fishmonger.

Once made, the stocks can be frozen when cooled. Freeze in small batches in plastic tubs or ice cube trays. When frozen, the cubes can be transferred to clearly labelled plastic bags for ease of storage.

A few basic rules are necessary when making stock.
• Stock should always simmer extremely gently, or it will evaporate too quickly and become cloudy.
• never add salt to the stock as simmering will reduce it and concentrate the flavour. This will affect the flavour of the finished dish.
• Any scum that rises to the surface should be removed as it will spoil the colour and flavour of the final stock.
• Avoid any floury root vegetables as these will cause the stock to become cloudy.

Beef stock

• Put 2.5 kg/5 lb beef or beef and veal bones in a roasting pan, and place in a preheated oven at 230°C/450°F/Gas Mark 8. Roast for 1 hour or until browned and the fat and juices run out. Using a slotted spoon, transfer the bones to a large pot.
• Place the roasting pan on top of the stove, add 2 onions roughly chopped, 2 carrots roughly chopped and 2 celery stalks roughly chopped. Fry gently in the remaining fat until nicely browned, but do not burn. Add the vegetables to the bones in the saucepan, together with 2 bay leaves, a few parsley stalks, 2 sprigs thyme, 10 whole peppercorns and cover with 4.8 litres/8 pints cold water.
• Bring to the boil, skim any scum from the surface, reduce the heat and simmer, uncovered, for 8 hours, skimming occasionally. Strain and cool, then refrigerate. Remove any surface fat on the surface.

Makes about 2.7 litres/4½ pints
Preparation time: 5–10 minutes
Cooking time: about 9 hours

• Place 1½ kg/3 lb fish trimmings and 1 onion, sliced, white part of a small leek, 1 celery stalk, 1 bay leaf, 6 parsley stalks, 10 whole peppercorns and 475 ml/16 fl oz dry white wine into a large pot, and cover with 1.8 litres/3 pints cold water. Bring slowly to just below boiling point. Simmer for 20 minutes, removing any scum from the surface. Strain the stock through a muslin-lined sieve and leave to cool before refrigerating.

Makes 1.8 litres/3 pints
Preparation time: 10 minutes
Cooking time: 20 minutes

Chicken stock

Chicken stock is used extensively in Chinese cooking, so a good recipe is essential. The following gives a light, delicately flavoured stock which has a good flavour, but will not overpower the ingredients in the final dish.

• Chop a cooked chicken carcass into 3 or 4 pieces and place it in a large pot with the raw giblets and trimmings, 1 onion roughly chopped, 2 large carrots roughly chopped, and 1 celery stalk roughly chopped, 1 bay leaf, a few parsley stalks, lightly crushed, 1 sprig thyme and cover with 1.8 litres/3 pints cold water.
• bring to the boil, removing any scum from the surface. Lower the heat and simmer for 2–2½ hours. Strain the stock through a muslin-lined sieve and leave to cool completely before refrigerating.

Makes 1 litre/1¾ pints
Preparation time: 5–10 minutes
Cooking time: about 2½ hours

Fish stock

When purchasing the bones for this stock, avoid buying the bones of oily fish. It is very important that the stock does not boil as it will become very cloudy.

Vegetable stock

This recipe makes a well-flavoured vegetable stock which makes a good basis for many recipes, and can also be varied to your own taste. Once you have made it several times, you might wish to experiment with other flavourings. You can also ring the changes according to which vegetables are in season at the time. Try adding some fennel bulb for a mild aniseed flavour, or a sliver of orange zest for an added lift. The addition of tomatoes will give it richness of flavour and colour. Avoid any floury root vegetables, however, as these will cause the stock to become cloudy.

• Place 500 g/1 lb chopped mixed vegetables ie.carrots, leeks, celery, onion and mushrooms, about an equal quantity of each; 1 clove garlic, 6 peppercorns, 1 bouquet garni (2 parsley sprigs, 2 sprigs thyme and 1 bay leaf) in a pan, and cover with 1.2 litres/2 pints water. Bring to the boil and simmer gently for 30 minutes, skimming when necessary. Strain the stock and cool it completely before refrigerating.

Makes 1 litre/1¾ pints
Preparation time: 5–10 minutes
Cooking time: about 45 minutes

Cook's tools

Good cooking does not depend on whether the dish is large or small, expensive or economical. If one has the art, then a piece of celery or salted cabbage can be made into a marvellous delicacy; whereas if one has not the art, not all the greatest delicacies and rarities of land and sea are of any avail.

Yuan Mei 18th century Chinese poet.

In Chinese cooking, kitchen tools are relatively basic. The emphasis tends to be on the preparation of food rather than the cooking, which often takes a very short time. This means that some items of equipment such as good quality knives are very important.

Bamboo steamer

The Chinese were probably the first people to discover the benefits of cooking by steam. Steaming food is an excellent way of maintaining the full nutritional value of the food and also ensuring that vitamin loss is kept to a minimum. Steaming food helps to maintain both colour and texture. The bamboo steamer allows different layers of food to be steamed over one pot of water, and can be used in conjunction with the wok.

Spatula

The spatula has a flexible, non-sharp blade set into a handle. In Chinese cooking the spatula is useful for moving food around a wok, especially when stir-frying. It can be made of stainless steel or plastic.

Chopsticks

Thousands of years before Western civilisation discovered knives and forks, the Chinese were using chopsticks to eat their food. The chopstick has changed very little in design since then, although these days they tend to be more ornate. They are still the best way to eat Chinese food, and can be made of wood, bamboo, plastic and silver. Ivory chopsticks are now a matter of controversy because of wildlife protection issues. They are also manufactured in bone derived from species that are not endangered.

Knives (chopping, paring, bread)

A good cook is not properly equipped without a set of kitchen knives. This is particularly the case in Chinese cooking, as vegetables and meat have to be cut so that just the right amount of surface area is exposed for correct cooking. Knives should be well maintained, cleaned and dried thoroughly and sharpened regularly.

Chopping knife: A heavy wide bladed knife ideal for chopping all vegetables and other ingredients, it is also good for flattening thinly sliced meats, and transferring ingredients from the board to the pan.

Paring knife: A small knife used for trimming and peeling vegetables.

Bread knife: A large serrated knife, good for slicing bread, cakes and pastries, as it stops the food from tearing.

Skimmer

A skimmer is a long handled, shallow metal spoon. It is perforated, so when it is used to remove food from the wok, any unwanted liquid will drain away.

Whisk

A whisk is an essential beating tool used to blend ingredients and incorporate air into batter or other mixtures. Whisks come in different shapes and sizes — small ones are used for sauces, though the larger balloon whisk is the most popular and commonly used. They are very handy for rescuing lumpy sauces.

Ladle

A shallow ladle is often used in Chinese cooking for adding liquid to the wok. It is also used for scooping out cooked food. Stainless steel is the best material for a ladle as wood or plastic ladles are easily scorched.

Chopstick rests

Chopstick rests are used in formal Chinese dinner settings. They allow chopsticks to be rested between courses without making a mess. They usually have ornate Chinese designs such as fish or dragons and are made of porcelain.

Soups and Starters

Hot and Sour Soup
with shrimps and mushrooms

Szechuan pickled vegetables are used to give this soup its special, hot-sour flavour. They are readily available in Chinese supermarkets.

4 dried Chinese mushrooms

2 celery sticks

900 ml/1½ pints Chicken Stock (see page 11)

175 g/6 oz shrimps, fresh or frozen and thawed

50 g/2 oz Szechuan pickled vegetables, sliced

50 g/2 oz canned bamboo shoots, drained and shredded

½ cucumber

2 tablespoons Chinese wine or sherry

2 tablespoons soy sauce

1 tablespoon red wine vinegar

25 g/1 oz ham, diced

1 spring onion, chopped

soak the dried mushrooms in warm water for 15 minutes. Squeeze dry, discard the hard stalks, then slice the mushroom caps.

slice the celery sticks diagonally.

bring the stock to the boil, add the shrimps, pickled vegetables, bamboo shoots, mushrooms and celery, and simmer for 5 minutes.

cut the cucumber into 5 cm/2 inch matchstick lengths. Add them to the pan with the Chinese wine or sherry, soy sauce, vinegar and ham, and cook for 1 minute.

sprinkle with the chopped spring onion and serve immediately.

Serves 4–6
Preparation time: *20 minutes*
Cooking time: *6–8 minutes*

Chicken Broth
with spareribs and shrimps

In China, the clear-simmering method is used to cook this delicate soup. It is traditionally made in an earthenware pot (called a sandpot) set over a low charcoal heat.

I meaty chicken carcass
750 g/1½ lb pork spareribs
500 g/1 lb ham, bacon or beef bones
2 litres/3½ pints water
2 teaspoons salt
2 teaspoons dried shrimps (optional)

put all the ingredients in a large, heavy pan or flameproof pot.

bring to the boil, cover and simmer gently for 1¾ hours, skimming off any scum frequently.

leave to cool. When cold, skim any fat from the surface.

reheat and serve as a soup or use as required.

Serves 6
Preparation time: *15 minutes*
Cooking time: *1¾–2¼ hours*

clipboard: In the West, the clear- simmering technique can be achieved by cooking in a heavy, flameproof casserole over a very low heat or in a cool oven. Few flavouring ingredients are used during cooking, which many people prefer, as they can then flavour their portion to taste. Spicy dips are usually served at the table to counteract the blandness of clear-simmered food. Sometimes clear-simmered food is quickly deep-fried before serving.

Spicy Chicken Soup

with garlic, turmeric and beanthread noodles

3 tablespoons sunflower oil
½ large onion, thinly sliced
2 garlic cloves, crushed
1 teaspoon fresh root ginger, chopped
½ teaspoon freshly ground black pepper
pinch of turmeric
175 g/6 oz cooked chicken, coarsely chopped
1 tablespoon light soy sauce
1 litre/1¾ pints Chicken Stock (see page 11)
a handful of beanthread noodles, soaked until soft
75 g/3 oz bean sprouts
spring onions, chopped, to garnish

heat the oil in a medium saucepan and fry the onion, garlic and ginger until the onion is soft.

add the pepper, turmeric and chicken and stir for 30 seconds.

add the soy sauce and stock and bring to the boil. Adjust the seasoning if necessary. Reduce the heat slightly and cook for 5 minutes.

drain the noodles. Divide them equally among 4 warmed soup bowls. Divide the bean sprouts among the bowls and pour the soup on top.

serve hot, garnished with chopped spring onions.

Serves 4
Preparation time: *15–20 minutes*
Cooking time: *15 minutes*

clipboard: Beanthread noodles, also called cellophane noodles, are made from mung bean flour. They must be soaked before cooking to make them soft.

Chicken and Sweetcorn Soup

with red pepper garnish

900 ml/1½ pints Chicken Stock (see page 11), with a
little of the cooked chicken reserved and chopped
350 g/12 oz sweetcorn kernels
2 teaspoons cornflour (optional)
1 tablespoon water (optional)
salt and pepper

To garnish

spring onions, chopped
or
½ red pepper, deseeded and chopped
into dice and strips

pour the stock into a large saucepan and add 250 g/8 oz of the sweetcorn.

bring to the boil, add salt and pepper to taste, cover and simmer for 15 minutes.

liquidize until smooth, then return to the pan.

reheat the soup. If it is not thick enough for your liking, blend the cornflour with the water to make a thin paste, stir into the soup and bring to the boil, stirring.

add the remaining sweetcorn and the reserved chopped chicken. Simmer for 5 minutes.

adjust the seasoning before serving, and garnish with the chopped spring onions, or red pepper, if liked.

Serves 4
Preparation time: *10 minutes*
Cooking time: *20–25 minutes*

Sweetcorn and Fish Soup *with ginger and spring onions*

500 g/1 lb white fish, such as cod or sea bass, filleted
1 teaspoon ginger juice, extracted from
fresh ginger root (see clipboard)
1 teaspoon Chinese wine or sherry
900 ml/1½ pints water
1 x 250 g/8 oz can sweetcorn, drained
1 teaspoon oil
1½ teaspoons cornflour, dissolved in 1 tablespoon
water
1 spring onion, chopped, to garnish
salt

place the fish in a shallow heatproof dish with the ginger juice, Chinese wine or sherry and a generous pinch of salt.

leave to marinate for 10 minutes.

place in a steamer and steam for 5–6 minutes. Remove from the heat and mash the fish with a fork. Set aside.

pour the water into a large saucepan and bring to the boil. Add the sweetcorn, oil and 1 teaspoon of salt. Simmer for 2 minutes.

add the cornflour mixture and cook, stirring, until the soup thickens.

add the fish and cook for 1 minute. Pour into soup bowls, sprinkle with spring onion and serve hot.

Serves 4–6
Preparation time: *15 minutes, plus 10 minutes marinating*
Cooking time: *about 15–20 minutes*

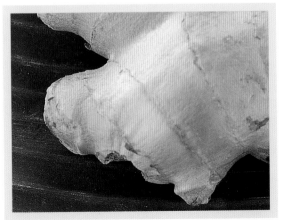

clipboard: Ginger juice can be extracted from the fresh root by placing small, peeled pieces in a garlic crusher, and squeezing firmly until you have the required amount.

Fish Soup
with coriander leaves

Fragrant coriander leaves — also known as Chinese parsley — add their pungent scent to this wonderfully aromatic fish soup.

250–375 g/8–12 oz fish fillets, such as sole, halibut, cod, bream, bass or carp, cut into 3.5 x 2.5 cm/1½ x 1 inch slices
1 teaspoon salt
1 tablespoon cornflour
900 ml/1½ pints Chicken Stock (see page 11)
2 slices root ginger, shredded
1 egg white, lightly beaten
3 tablespoons red wine vinegar
½ teaspoon pepper
1½ tablespoons coriander leaves, chopped

rub the fish slices with the salt and cornflour.

bring the stock to the boil in a pan. Add the ginger, then taste and add salt if necessary.

dip the fish slices in the beaten egg white, then add them to the stock, a few at a time.

return the stock to the boil, then lower the heat and simmer gently for 5 minutes, or until the fish is tender.

sprinkle the soup with the vinegar, pepper and coriander leaves. Stir a few times, then transfer to a serving tureen. Serve hot.

Serves 4
Preparation time: *20 minutes*
Cooking time: *20–30 minutes*

clipboard: The use of a lightly seasoned chicken stock in this soup gives it a delicate flavour, so try to avoid using a stock cube if possible.

Prawn and Squid Hot Soup

For a really warming, spicy start to a meal, there is nothing to beat this mouthwatering soup. It is packed with the aromatic tastes of lemon grass, chillies and coriander

250 g/8 oz squid, cleaned
1.8 litres/3 pints Chicken Stock (see page 11)
3 lime leaves
1 stem lemon grass, crushed
250 g/8 oz uncooked prawns, peeled
nam pla, to taste
2–4 fresh chillies, deseeded, sliced into rounds
2 garlic cloves, crushed
juice of 1 lime or 1 lemon
coriander leaves, freshly chopped, to garnish

prepare the squid: hold the head and tentacles in one hand and pull away the body with the other. Pull the innards and the hard 'pen' away from the body and discard. Cut the tentacles from the head. Scrape the thin skin from the body and tentacles. Rinse well and pat dry. Cut the squid into rings.

put the stock, lime leaves and lemon grass in a pan and bring to the boil. Reduce the heat and simmer for 5 minutes. Add the prawns, squid and *nam pla*. Cook until the prawns turn pink. Add the chillies.

pour the soup into 4 warmed individual bowls. Mix together the garlic and lime or lemon juice, and stir into the soup. Sprinkle with chopped coriander and serve hot.

Serves 4–6
Preparation time: *15 minutes, plus 10 minutes marinating*
Cooking time: *about 15–20 minutes*

clipboard: *Nam pla* is a salty, spiced, fermented fish mixture, available from oriental food stores.

Coin Purse Eggs
with fresh coriander

*This Szechuan dish acquired its evocative name
because the folded-over eggs are thought to resemble
purses containing golden coins.*

6 tablespoons sunflower oil

8 eggs

3 tablespoons light soy sauce

2 tablespoons white wine vinegar

4 tablespoons coriander or parsley, chopped (optional)

salt and pepper

heat 2 tablespoons of the oil in a frying pan over a moderate heat. Break in 1 egg, getting the yolk to one side, if possible.

add salt and pepper. Fry until the underside is set. Fold over one side of the white to cover the yolk completely.

increase the heat and cook until the underside is golden brown. Turn the egg over carefully and brown the other side.

transfer the egg to a warmed serving dish and keep warm.

cook the remaining eggs in the same way.

mix together the soy sauce and vinegar, and sprinkle over the eggs. Scatter the chopped herbs, if using, on top and serve with any stir-fry of your choice.

Serves 4
Preparation time: *5 minutes*
Cooking time: *15–20 minutes*

Green Peppers
stuffed with pork and ginger

1 tablespoon sunflower oil
1 garlic clove, crushed
1 piece fresh root ginger, peeled and finely chopped
250 g/8 oz lean minced pork
1 spring onion, chopped
1 celery stick, finely chopped
rind of 1 lemon, grated
4 green peppers

heat the oil in a wok or frying pan over a moderate heat. Add the garlic and stir-fry until lightly browned.

reduce the heat and add the ginger and pork. Stir-fry for 2 minutes.

add the spring onion, celery and lemon rind. Combine well and stir-fry for another 30 seconds. Let the mixture cool slightly.

cut the peppers into quarters and remove the core and seeds.

divide the mixture between the 4 quarters, pressing it down into each of the cavities.

arrange the pepper quarters in an oiled, ovenproof dish. Cook in a preheated oven at 200°C/400°F/Gas Mark 6 for 25 minutes, until tender.

transfer to a warmed serving dish and serve immediately.

Serves 4-6
Preparation time: *15 minutes*
Cooking time: *30–35 minutes*
Oven temperature: *200°C/400°F/Gas Mark 6*

clipboard: If you are using a new wok for the first time, you must remove the protective film of oil. Heat the wok over high heat until very hot, then scrub it with warm soapy water. Rinse and dry over moderate heat. Season the wok by wiping it with a pad of absorbent kitchen paper soaked in cooking oil. Wash without detergent after each use.

Fish and Seafood

Scallop and Prawn
stir-fry with mixed vegetables

4–6 fresh scallops

125–175 g/4–6 oz uncooked prawns, heads removed, defrosted if frozen

1 egg white

1 tablespoon cornflour

3 celery sticks, trimmed

1 red pepper, cored and deseeded

1–2 carrots, peeled

2 slices fresh root ginger, peeled

2–3 spring onions

600 ml/1 pint vegetable oil for deep-frying

2 tablespoons Chinese wine or dry sherry

1 tablespoon light soy sauce

2 teaspoons chilli bean paste (optional)

1 teaspoon salt

1 teaspoon sesame seed oil, to finish

cut each scallop into 3–4 pieces. Peel the prawns, and remove the black vein. Leave them whole if small, otherwise cut each one into 2 or 3 pieces. Put the seafood in a bowl with the egg white and about half of the cornflour and mix together.

cut the celery, red pepper and carrots into small pieces. Finely shred the ginger and spring onions.

heat the oil in a hot wok, then deep-fry the scallops and prawns for 1 minute, stirring them all the time with chopsticks to keep the pieces separate. Scoop them out with a perforated spoon and drain on absorbent kitchen paper.

pour off all but 2 tablespoons oil from the wok. Increase the heat to high and add the ginger and spring onions. Add the vegetables and stir-fry for about 1 minute, then return the scallops and prawns to the wok and stir in the wine or sherry, soy sauce and chilli bean paste (if using), and season with the salt.

mix the remaining cornflour to a smooth paste with a little stock or water, then add to the wok and blend all the ingredients until thickened. Sprinkle over the sesame seed oil and serve immediately.

Serves 4–6
Preparation time: *20–25 minutes*
Cooking time: *6–8 minutes*

Szechuan Prawns
in chilli and tomato sauce

This is a typical Szechuan dish — hot, peppery and richly flavoured with chilli sauce.

250 g/8 oz raw prawns, peeled
1 egg white
2 teaspoons cornflour
sunflower oil for deep-frying
1 spring onion, finely chopped
2 slices fresh root ginger, peeled and finely chopped
1 garlic clove, finely chopped
1 tablespoon Chinese wine or dry sherry
1 tablespoon tomato purée
1 tablespoon chilli sauce
lettuce leaves
salt
tomato rose, to garnish (optional)

mix a pinch of the salt with the prawns, add the egg white and dust with cornflour.

heat the oil in a wok or deep pan. Add the prawns, stirring to keep them separate, and deep-fry for 30 seconds over moderate heat.

remove from the wok and drain.

pour off all but 1 tablespoon of oil from the wok. Over a high heat, stir-fry the spring onion, ginger and garlic for a few seconds.

add the prawns and stir-fry for 1 minute. Add the wine, tomato purée and chilli sauce, stirring until the sauce is well blended.

line a dish with lettuce and pour the prawns and sauce into the centre. Serve immediately, garnished with a tomato rose, if liked.

Serves 4
Preparation time: *20–25 minutes*
Cooking time: *5 minutes*

clipboard: To make a tomato rose, remove the skin in one continuous strip about 1 cm/½ inch wide. With the flesh side inside, curl it from the base end, forming a flower shape.

Deep-fried Prawn Cutlets

in a light, crispy batter

8 Dublin Bay or Pacific prawns
1 tablespoon Chinese wine or dry sherry
1 egg, beaten
2 tablespoons cornflour
oil for deep frying
sprig of coriander (optional)

hold the prawns firmly by the tail and remove the shell, leaving the tail shell piece intact.

cut the prawns in half lengthways almost through to the tail, and remove the dark intestinal vein.

flatten the prawns with a light wooden mallet to resemble cutlets. Sprinkle with the Chinese rice wine or sherry.

dip the cutlets in beaten egg, then in the cornflour, and then repeat. Heat the oil to 180°C/350°F.

deep-fry the prawns for 2–3 minutes. Drain them thoroughly on absorbent kitchen paper.

arrange on a serving plate and garnish with fresh coriander, if liked. Serve plain or with sweet soy bean paste.

Serves 2
Preparation time: *20 minutes*
Cooking time: *2–3 minutes*

clipboard: Rice wine is made from fermented rice and is sold in Chinese supermarkets. You can use dry sherry as a substitute.

Scrambled Eggs
with prawns and beansprouts

Crisp, firm, beansprouts add texture to the fresh eggs and prawns, making this a deliciously healthy, easy-to-prepare dish.

8 eggs
3 tablespoons soy sauce
4 tablespoons oil
2 medium onions, thinly sliced
1 garlic clove, finely chopped
150 g/5 oz beansprouts
125 g/4 oz shelled prawns

beat the eggs with the soy sauce.

heat the oil in a wok or large frying pan on a high heat.

put in the onions, garlic and beansprouts and stir-fry for 1 minute.

mix in the eggs and the prawns. Cook, stirring constantly, until the eggs set to a scramble.

Serves 4
Preparation time: *10 minutes*
Cooking time: *5–6 minutes*

clipboard: Beansprouts are the sprouts of small green mung beans. Although they are available in cans, it is best to use them as fresh as possible. They are widely available in supermarkets and grocery stores. You can grow your own beansprouts by putting some mung beans in a jam jar. Cover with a piece of muslin and secure with an elastic band. Rinse the beans every day until the sprouts are long enough.

Stir-fried Crab
with ginger and spring onion

Fresh crabs are a favourite ingredient in Chinese cooking. If you are unsure about preparing them, you can ask your fishmonger to do this for you.

1 x 875 g/1½ lb crab
2 tablespoons Chinese wine or dry sherry
1 tablespoon Chicken Stock (see page 11) or water
2 tablespoons cornflour
4 slices fresh ginger root, peeled and finely chopped
4 spring onions, finely chopped
3 tablespoons sunflower oil
1 teaspoon salt
1 tablespoon light soy sauce
2 teaspoons sugar

wash the crab shells and separate the legs and claws. Crack the claws with the back of a cleaver.

crack the shells into 2–3 pieces. Discard the feathery gills and the sac.

place the crab in a bowl with 1 tablespoon of the wine or sherry, the stock or water and the cornflour.

stir once or twice and leave to marinate for 10 minutes.

combine the chopped ginger and spring onion.

heat the oil in a wok or frying pan until it is hot, then add the crab pieces and stir-fry for 1 minute.

add the ginger and onion, the salt, soy sauce, sugar and remaining wine or sherry. Cook for about 5 minutes, stirring constantly.

add a little water if the mixture becomes very dry. Serve hot.

Serves 4
Preparation time: *25–30 minutes, plus 10 minutes marinating*
Cooking time: *6 minutes*

Quick-fried Crab
in aromatic oil with garlic

Because stir-frying is done so rapidly, the cooking oil is often scented with aromatic flavourings first — with garlic and ginger, as in this recipe, or with chillies.

1 x 875 g/1½lb crab, freshly cooked
2 tablespoons sunflower oil
1 clove garlic, crushed
2 pieces root ginger, finely chopped
4 spring onions, chopped
1 leek, thinly sliced
1 egg, beaten
150 ml/ ¼ pint Fish Stock or Chicken Stock (see page 11)
2 tablespoons Chinese wine or dry sherry
2 teaspoons cornflour, blended with 1 tablespoon water
salt
1 teaspoon sesame oil, to finish
lemon wedges, to garnish

break off the legs and crack the claws of the crab. Using a chopper, crack the shell into 4–5 pieces.

remove all the meat and cut into pieces, discarding the black sac and intestinal thread.

heat the oil in a wok or frying pan, add the garlic, ginger and spring onions and stir-fry for 1 minute.

add the crab and stir-fry for 5 minutes over a high heat. Add the leek and salt to taste.

lower the heat and pour in the egg in a thin stream. Add the stock and wine or sherry and cook for 1 minute.

add the cornflour and sesame oil; cook, stirring, until thickened.

turn on to a warmed serving dish and serve the crab immediately, garnished with lemon wedges.

Serves 4–6
Preparation time: *about 20 minutes*
Cooking time: *7–10 minutes*

Stir-fried Fish
with bacon and mixed vegetables

If you prefer, you can use any good quality, firm white fish in this recipe. Unsmoked haddock is excellent, for example. Check with your fishmonger to see what is available.

500 g/1 lb cod fillet, skinned and cut into wide strips
1 teaspoon salt
1 tablespoon oil
2 rashers back bacon, shredded
50 g/2 oz peas, cooked
50 g/2 oz sweetcorn kernels, cooked
6 tablespoons Chicken Stock (see page 11) or water
2 teaspoons Chinese wine or dry sherry
2 teaspoons light soy sauce
1 teaspoon sugar
1 teaspoon cornflour
1 teaspoon water

To garnish
lemon slices (optional)
spring onions

sprinkle the fish fillets with the salt and leave to stand for 15 minutes.

heat the oil in a wok or frying pan over a moderate heat.

add the fish and bacon and stir-fry for 3 minutes.

add the remaining ingredients, except the cornflour and water, and bring to the boil.

blend the cornflour with the water to make a thin paste and add to the sauce. Stir and cook for 1 minute.

serve hot, garnished with lemon slices, if using, and spring onions.

Serves 4
Preparation time: *5 minutes, plus 15 minutes standing*
Cooking time: *5–7 minutes*

Mixed Seafood
with stick noodles and ginger

4 dried Chinese mushrooms
500 g/1 lb rice noodles
2 tablespoons oil
4 spring onions, chopped
2 cloves garlic, sliced
1 piece root ginger, finely chopped
50 g/2 oz frozen peeled prawns, thawed
125 g/4 oz fresh or frozen squid, sliced (optional)
1 x 250 g/8 oz can clams, drained
2 tablespoons Chinese wine or dry sherry
1 tablespoon soy sauce
salt

soak the mushrooms in warm water for 15 minutes. Squeeze well, discard the stalks, then slice the mushroom caps.

cook the rice stick noodles in boiling salted water for 7–8 minutes until they are just tender.

drain and rinse in cold water. Keep on one side.

heat the oil in a wok or deep frying pan, add the spring onions, garlic and ginger and stir-fry for 30 seconds.

stir in the mushrooms, prawns and squid, if you are using them, then cook for 2 minutes.

stir in the remaining ingredients, then carefully stir in the noodles and heat through.

pile the mixture into a warmed serving dish and serve immediately.

Serves 4–6
Preparation time: *10 minutes, plus 15 minutes soaking*
Cooking time: *10–11 minutes*

clipboard: Chinese dried mushrooms have a delicious, strong flavour, but they must be soaked for 15–20 minutes before using. They are available from Chinese supermarkets, but if you cannot obtain them, use Continental dried mushrooms instead.

Stir-fried Squid
with green peppers and ginger

250 g/8 oz squid
sunflower oil for deep-frying
2 slices fresh root ginger, peeled and thinly sliced
125 g/4 oz green peppers, deseeded and sliced
1 teaspoon salt
1 tablespoon light soy sauce
1 teaspoon wine vinegar
1 teaspoon sesame oil
pepper

prepare the squid: hold the head and tentacles in one hand and pull away the body with the other.

pull the innards and the hard 'pen' away from the body and discard. Cut the tentacles from the head.

scrape the thin skin from the body and tentacles. Rinse well and pat dry. Cut the flesh into small pieces the size of a matchbox.

heat the oil over moderate heat in a wok or frying pan and deep-fry the squid for about 30 seconds, stirring with chopsticks to prevent the pieces sticking together.

pour off all but 1 tablespoon of oil from the wok. Add the ginger, green peppers and squid and stir-fry for 1 minute.

add the salt, soy sauce, vinegar and pepper and stir-fry for 1 minute. Add the sesame oil and serve hot.

Serves 4
Preparation time: *20 minutes*
Cooking time: *about 5 minutes*

clipboard: If you do not wish to clean the squid yourself, you can buy it ready-prepared at the fresh fish counter of large supermarkets. It is certainly convenient to buy it this way if you do not have much time. Try to get the smallest squid available, as they will be the most tender.

Baby Squid
stir-fried with fresh, green herbs

1 kg/2 lb baby squid
4 tablespoons sunflower oil
3–4 cloves garlic, sliced
2 tablespoons coriander, freshly chopped
1 tablespoon flat-leaf parsley, freshly chopped
juice of ½ lemon
salt and pepper

prepare the squid: hold the head and tentacles in one hand and pull away the body with the other.

pull the innards and the hard 'pen' away from the body and discard. Cut the tentacles from the head.

scrape the thin skin from the body and tentacles. Rinse well and pat dry. Cut the flesh into slices. Season with salt and pepper to taste.

heat the oil in a wok over gentle heat. Add the garlic slices and cook until browned. Remove with a slotted spoon and discard.

increase the heat. When the oil is hot, add the squid and cook briskly for 1 minute, stirring to prevent the pieces sticking together.

add the coriander, parsley and lemon juice and stir-fry for 30 seconds. Transfer to a warmed serving dish.

serve immediately, garnished with slices of lemon or lime, and tiny sprigs of fresh herbs.

Serves 4
Preparation time: *about 10 minutes*
Cooking time: *2–4 minutes*

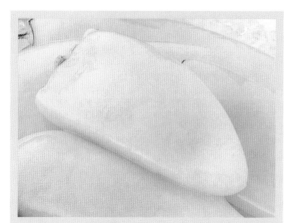

clipboard: Squid must be cooked quickly or the flesh becomes tough. Consequently, it is ideal for stir-fried dishes such as this. Baby squid is the best to use for stir-frying, as its flesh is delicate and very tender.

Braised Fish
with vegetables in black bean sauce

Colourful, fragrant and fresh-tasting, this is a perfect way to prepare fish. The black beans make a wonderful sauce, and provide great colour contrast.

3 tablespoons salted black beans
2 tablespoons oil
2 spring onions, chopped
1 x 2.5 cm/1 inch piece fresh root ginger, peeled and chopped
1 small red pepper, cored, deseeded and chopped
2 celery sticks, chopped
2 tablespoons light soy sauce
2 tablespoons Chinese wine or dry sherry
4 x 150 g/5 oz cod or haddock cutlets
spring onion, shredded, to garnish

soak the black beans in warm water for 10 minutes. Drain.

heat the oil in a wok or deep frying pan. Add the spring onions, ginger, red pepper and celery and stir-fry for 1 minute.

stir in the soy sauce and wine or sherry. Place the fish on top of the vegetables and simmer for about 5–10 minutes, depending on the thickness of the fish. Cook until almost tender.

spoon over the black beans and cook for 2 minutes.

arrange the fish on a warmed serving dish and spoon the sauce over. Serve hot, garnished with shredded spring onion.

Serves 4
Preparation time: *20 minutes*
Cooking time: *10–15 minutes*

clipboard: Black beans are salted and fermented and have a very strong salty flavour. They are sold in polythene bags or cans in Chinese food stores, and will keep almost indefinitely, but they must always be soaked for 5–10 minutes before cooking.

Deep-fried Sole
with herbs and satay sauce

If possible, use Dover sole for this recipe, as it has a particularly fine flavour. It is expensive, so if you want a good alternative, use lemon sole.

I teaspoon each of coriander, cumin
and fennel seeds, crushed
2 garlic cloves, crushed
125 g/4 oz crunchy peanut butter
I teaspoon dark soft brown sugar
2 fresh green chillies, deseeded, chopped
150 g/5 oz creamed coconut
450 ml/¾ pint water
3 tablespoons lemon juice
25 g/I oz butter
I shallot, finely chopped
I tablespoon each of chives, tarragon
and parsley, chopped
grated rind of ½ lemon
8 Dover or lemon sole fillets
I egg, beaten
4–5 tablespoons fresh breadcrumbs
sunflower oil for deep-frying
sprigs of flat-leaved parsley, to garnish

make the sauce: heat a wok, add the spice seeds and stir-fry for 2 minutes. Add the garlic, peanut butter, sugar and chillies.

combine the creamed coconut with the water and stir it in. Cook gently for 7–8 minutes. Stir in the lemon juice.

melt the butter in a pan, add the shallot and cook for 1 minute. Stir in the herbs and lemon rind. Cool slightly.

pour this mixture over the fish fillets. Roll up each one and secure with wooden cocktail sticks.

dip in the egg, coat in breadcrumbs, and deep-fry in hot oil for 4–5 minutes until golden.

drain and serve, garnished with a sprig of parsley, with the sauce handed separately.

Serves 4
Preparation time: *35 minutes*
Cooking time: *15–20 minutes*

clipboard: Creamed coconut is sold in blocks, which should be softened in boiling water before use. Coconut powder, mixed to a paste with water, is an acceptable alternative.

Rainbow Trout
steamed in aromatic seasonings

What could be nicer than these delicate, beautifully flavoured trout. Steaming is one of the healthiest ways to cook — no fat is required, and the taste of the food is perfectly preserved.

1 tablespoon sesame oil
1 tablespoon light soy sauce
1 tablespoon Chinese wine or dry sherry
2 rainbow trout, weighing about
1 kg/2 lb in total, cleaned
4 garlic cloves, sliced
6 spring onions, shredded
1 x 5 cm/2 inch piece fresh root ginger,
peeled and shredded
2 tablespoons dry white vermouth
2 tablespoons sunflower oil

mix together the sesame oil, soy sauce and wine or sherry and use to brush the inside and skin of the fish.

mix together the garlic, spring onions and ginger, and place a quarter of this mixture inside each fish.

place the fish on a heatproof plate, scatter over the remaining garlic mixture and pour over the vermouth and oil.

put the plate in a wok or steamer and steam vigorously for 15 minutes, or until the fish are tender.

arrange the cooked trout on a warmed serving dish, pour over the juices and serve at once.

Serves 4
Preparation time: *10 minutes*
Cooking time: *15–20 minutes*

clipboard: Traditional Chinese bamboo steamers are decorative as well as practical. They are designed so that they can be stacked on top of one another, allowing different foods to be steamed at the same time. They are available from Chinese supermarkets.

Fish Parcels
deep-fried and wrapped in paper

4 x 125 g/4 oz fillets of sole or plaice
pinch of salt
2 tablespoons Chinese wine or dry sherry
1 tablespoon vegetable oil
2 tablespoons spring onion, shredded
2 tablespoons fresh root ginger, shredded
extra vegetable oil for deep frying
spring onion tassels, to garnish

cut the fish fillets into 2.5 cm/1 inch squares. Sprinkle with the salt and toss them in the wine or sherry.

cut out 15 cm/6 inch squares of greaseproof paper and brush them lightly with the oil.

place a piece of fish on each square of paper and arrange some shredded spring onion and ginger on top.

fold the pieces of paper into envelopes tucking in the flaps firmly to secure them.

heat the oil in a wok or deep saucepan to 180°C/350°F or until a cube of day-old bread browns in 30 seconds. Deep-fry the wrapped fish parcels for 3 minutes.

drain and arrange on a warmed serving dish. Garnish with spring onion tassels and serve at once. Each person at the table unwraps their own fish parcels with chopsticks.

Serves 4
Preparation time: *15 minutes*
Cooking time: *3–5 minutes*

clipboard: Spring onion tassels are a popular Chinese garnish. Trim a 7.5 cm (3 inch) piece of the green stalk. Reserve the white bulb for another use. Finely shred the top leaves, leaving 2.5cm (1 inch) attached at the base. Immerse in iced water until the tassel opens out and curls.

Fish Steaks

with soy sauce and ginger

Choose a robust white fish with a firm texture for this dish, as it will combine well with the rich, dark colour and pungent flavour of the soy sauce.

500 g/1 lb fish steak, such as cod, halibut, monkfish or hake

½ teaspoon salt

2 tablespoons Chinese wine or sherry

4 tablespoons cornflour

1 egg white, lightly beaten

3 tablespoons sunflower oil

1 slice fresh root ginger, peeled and finely chopped

2 tablespoons light soy sauce

2 teaspoons sugar

125 ml/4 fl oz Chicken Stock (see page 11) or water

spring onion, to garnish

cut the fish steak into pieces about the size of a matchbox.

mix together the salt, wine or sherry and 1 tablespoon of the cornflour, and marinate the fish in this mixture for about 30 minutes.

dip the fish pieces in egg white, then in the remaining cornflour.

heat the oil in a wok or frying pan until hot, then fry the fish pieces until golden, stirring them gently to separate each piece.

add the ginger, soy sauce, sugar and stock or water. Cook for 3–4 minutes, or until the liquid has completely evaporated.

serve hot, garnished with spring onion.

Serves 4
Preparation time: *about 15 minutes, plus 30 minutes marinating*
Cooking time: *15–20 minutes*

clipboard: This method of coating fish in egg white and cornflour before putting it in the hot oil is an excellent way of preventing the fish from breaking up during stir-frying.

Young Spinach
with cockles and mustard sauce

Next time you find a supply of cockles at your fishmonger, try this Chinese method of cooking them. It is a perfectly delicious recipe for this familiar shellfish.

1 tablespoon Chinese wine or dry sherry
250 g/8 oz cockles, cleaned
3 tablespoons soy sauce, plus 1 teaspoon
1 teaspoon hot mustard
500 g/1 lb tender young spinach leaves, washed and trimmed
salt
1 tablespoon sesame seeds, to garnish

heat the rice wine or sherry in a small saucepan. Add the cockles and heat through. Drain, reserving the liquid.

mix 3 tablespoons of the soy sauce in a bowl with the mustard, then add the cleaned cockles.

blanch the spinach leaves in lightly salted boiling water for 30 seconds. Drain and immediately plunge the leaves into a bowl of ice-cold water.

drain the spinach again and squeeze out any excess water. Pour over 1 teaspoon soy sauce.

add the reserved liquid to the cockle mixture. Arrange the spinach on a serving plate.

place the cockle mixture in the centre and garnish with sesame seeds. Serve at once.

Serves 4
Preparation time: *15 minutes*
Cooking time: *about 5 minutes*

clipboard: Sorrel or rocket are good alternatives to spinach, but if you use them, they need not be blanched.

Sauces

Black bean sauce

Hoisin sauce

Yellow bean sauce

Chilli sauce

Light soy sauce

Yellow bean sauce

Yellow bean sauce is made from yellow soya beans. It is more of a paste than a sauce, and very similar in taste to soy sauce. Sold in bottles, it is sometimes used as a substitute for soy sauce, as it is thicker, and produces a richer sauce in cooking. Yellow bean sauce is now easily available in the larger supermarkets.

Black bean sauce

Black bean sauce is a thick, black sauce made from black soya beans. It can be used by itself as a savoury dip or incorporated into stir-fried, braised, or fish dishes. Black bean sauce is easily made at home — a quick method is to blend sugar, garlic and soy sauce to taste, together with a rinsed can of salted black beans.

Chilli sauce

Chilli sauce is a rich red sauce with a hot spicy taste. It is made from red chillies and can be used with all types of Chinese cooking either by itself or as a dip. Mostly it is sparingly incorporated into a dish, but chilli sauce is generously employed in Szechuan cooking, which is renowned for its hot, spicy dishes.

Light soy sauce

Light soy sauce has a delicate, mildly salty flavour, and is distinctly lighter in colour than traditional soy sauce. The colour of any sauce is dependent on the length of time that it has been aged. Soy sauce is used in Chinese cooking, in seafood dishes, soups and also as a dipping sauce.

Hoisin sauce

One of the most commonly used Chinese sauces is hoisin, available from supermarkets and Chinese stores. It is used for grilling and barbecuing, and is also served separately as a dipping sauce. It is made from soya beans, tomato purée and spices. It is best known for its use in Chinese barbecued spare ribs.

Spices

Szechuan pepper

Five-spice powder

Star anise

Cinnamon

Chilli powder

Cloves

Star anise

Star anise is the dried, star-shaped pod of a variety of magnolia tree, native to Southern China. The prettily shaped spice is widely used as a flavouring in Chinese cooking, and its strong aniseed flavour complements various meat and poultry dishes. Star anise is one of the spices used in five-spice powder.

Chilli powder

Chilli powder is dark red in colour and is used in spicy dishes for its hot and peppery flavour. Depending on the type of chilli used, it can vary considerably in strength so it is a good idea to be careful when adding it to food. You might try tasting a tiny portion on the tip of the finger to get an idea of its strength.

Szechuan pepper

Szechuan pepper is also known as Chinese pepper, but it is not a true pepper. The pungent corns are the dried berries of a Chinese shrub. The pepper is very fragrant and has a strong, distinctive flavour, although it is not very hot. The corns are roasted prior to grinding. It is an ingredient in five-spice powder.

Cinnamon

Cinnamon is a light brown spice, with a strong, sweet aroma. It is frequently used in soups, baking, liqueurs and flavoured oils.

Five-spice powder

Five-spice powder is a fragrant spice mixture which has long been a traditional ingredient in Chinese cooking. In fact there are often more than five spices used to make up the powder, but the main ingredients are star anise, Szechuan pepper, cinnamon, cloves, and fennel seeds.

Cloves

Cloves are from Indonesia and are fragrant with a fruity, slightly bitter flavour. They are used in sweet and savoury dishes.

Chicken and Poultry

Sweet Chicken Wings *braised with oyster sauce and ginger*

500 g/1 lb chicken wings
3 tablespoons oyster sauce
1 tablespoon soy sauce
300 ml/½ pint Chicken Stock (see page 11)
pinch of salt
1 teaspoon brown sugar
25 g/1 oz root ginger, finely chopped
pinch of black pepper
1 teaspoon coarse salt
spring onion, finely sliced, to garnish

put the chicken wings into a pan with just enough cold water to cover.

bring to the boil, cover and simmer for 10 minutes.

drain and discard the water.

put the chicken wings back into the pan and add the oyster sauce, soy sauce, stock, salt and sugar.

bring slowly to the boil, cover and simmer for 20 minutes.

sprinkle the ginger, pepper and coarse salt over the chicken. Serve hot, garnished with fine strips of spring onion.

Serves 4
Preparation time: *10 minutes*
Cooking time: *30 minutes*

clipboard: Oyster sauce is widely used in Chinese cooking to flavour poultry, meat and vegetables. Used mainly in the South of China, it is made from an extract of oysters and soy sauce. Oyster sauce is sold in bottles at Chinese foodstores and at some large supermarkets.

Stir-fried Lemon Chicken *with vegetables*

375 g/12 oz chicken off the bone, skin removed
2 tablespoons Chinese wine or dry sherry
4 spring onions, chopped
1 x 2.5 cm/1 inch piece fresh root ginger,
peeled and finely chopped
2 tablespoons sunflower oil
1–2 garlic cloves, sliced
2 celery sticks, sliced diagonally
1 small green pepper, cored, deseeded
and sliced lengthways
2 tablespoons light soy sauce
juice of ½ lemon
rind of 2 lemons, shredded
¼ teaspoon chilli powder

To garnish (optional)
lemon slices
sprig of parsley

cut the chicken into 7 cm/3 inch strips. Mix the wine or sherry with the spring onions and ginger.

add the chicken and toss well to coat the pieces. Set aside to marinate for 15 minutes.

heat the oil in a wok or frying pan and add the garlic, celery and green pepper. Stir-fry for 1 minute.

add the chicken in its marinade and cook for a further 2 minutes.

stir in the soy sauce, lemon juice and rind and the chilli powder, and cook for 1 minute more.

transfer to a warmed serving dish and garnish with lemon slices and a sprig of fresh parsley, if liked.

Serves 4
Preparation time: *5 minutes, plus 15 minutes marinating*
Cooking time: *4 minutes*

Stir-fried Chicken
with shiitake mushrooms

25 g/1 oz dried shiitake mushrooms
5 tablespoons sunflower oil
2 garlic cloves, crushed
250 g/8 oz boneless chicken breast, cut into strips
50 g/2 oz baby corn cobs, blanched
175 ml/6 fl oz Chicken Stock (see page 11)
1 tablespoon *nam pla*
generous pinch of salt
generous pinch of sugar
½ tablespoon cornflour
2 tablespoons water

soak the dried mushrooms in warm water to cover for 5 minutes. Discard the stems and cut the caps into quarters.

heat the oil in a wok or large frying pan. Add the garlic and cook over moderate heat until golden.

add the chicken and stir-fry for 10 minutes. Lift out and set aside.

add the mushrooms and baby corn to the oil remaining in the wok. Stir-fry for 1-2 minutes.

stir in the chicken stock and bring to the boil. Reduce the heat, return the chicken to the wok and season with *nam pla*, salt and sugar.

simmer for 10 minutes or until the chicken is tender and the liquid is reduced by about half.

mix the cornflour with the water to make a thin paste. Add to the chicken mixture and cook, stirring constantly, until the sauce thickens. Serve immediately.

Serves 4
Preparation time: *15 minutes, plus 5 minutes soaking*
Cooking time: *30 minutes*

clipboard: Dried shiitake mushrooms are sold in small packets at oriental food stores. They have an earthy, highly concentrated flavour, and are therefore used in small quantities.

Stewed Chicken

with chestnuts and ginger

*Chicken has a special compatibility with the flavour
of chestnuts, as this recipe demonstrates so successfully.*

6 tablespoons soy sauce

1 tablespoon Chinese wine or dry sherry

1 x 1 kg/2 lb chicken, boned and cut into
3.5 cm/1½ inch pieces

2 tablespoons oil

2 slices root ginger, chopped

4 spring onions, chopped

500 g/1 lb chestnuts, peeled and skinned

450 ml/¾ pint water

1 tablespoon sugar

mix together the soy sauce and wine or sherry in a dish and add the chicken. Leave to marinate for 15 minutes.

heat the oil in a large pan. Add the chicken mixture, ginger and half the spring onions. Stir-fry until the chicken is golden.

add the chestnuts, water and sugar. Bring to the boil, cover and simmer for 40 minutes or until tender.

serve hot, garnished with the remaining spring onions.

Serves 3–4
Preparation time: *10 minutes, plus 15 minutes marinating*
Cooking time: *50 minutes–1 hour*

clipboard: If fresh chestnuts are not available, canned or dried ones may be used instead. Canned chestnuts should be drained and added to the chicken mixture 10 minutes before the end of the cooking time. If dried chestnuts are used, they should be soaked in warm water overnight before using, then cooked as for fresh chestnuts.

Braised Chicken
with red peppers and ginger

3 tablespoons oil

3 red peppers, cored, deseeded and sliced into rings

I teaspoon salt

2 tablespoons water

500 g/I lb chicken meat, cut into

2.5 cm/I inch pieces

25 g/I oz root ginger, finely chopped

pinch of brown sugar

2 teaspoons Chinese wine or dry sherry

I teaspoon cornflour

2 teaspoons soy sauce

heat 1 tablespoon of the oil in a pan. Add the pepper rings and salt.

stir-fry for 1 minute, then add the water and simmer gently until the liquid has evaporated.

remove the peppers from the pan and set aside.

heat the remaining oil in the pan. Add the chicken and ginger, and stir-fry for 1 minute. Stir in the sugar and wine or sherry.

dissolve the cornflour in the soy sauce and add to the pan. Simmer, stirring, until thickened.

add the pepper rings and cook for 1 minute. Serve hot.

Serves 4
Preparation time: *15 minutes*
Cooking time: *40 minutes*

clipboard: Chinese recipes often require finely chopped ginger root. Here is a useful technique for doing this. Peel the piece of root, and trim both ends flat. Stand on one end, and make a line of vertical cuts with a sharp knife. Holding the cut root together, turn it at right angles. Cut through again, making lines of fine strips. These can then be neatly chopped into small squares.

Steamed Chicken
with Chinese cabbage

1 x 1.5 kg/3 lb chicken
2 teaspoons salt
6–8 dried shiitake mushrooms
750 g/1½ lb Chinese cabbage
5 slices fresh root ginger, peeled
2 chicken stock cubes
coriander leaves, to garnish

bring a large saucepan of water to the boil. Add the salt and immerse the chicken in the water. Skim off all scum that rises to the surface and boil for 5–6 minutes. Drain the chicken.

soak the mushrooms in boiling water and leave to stand for 20 minutes. Drain and discard the stems. Cut the cabbage into 5 cm/2 inch slices.

place the mushroom caps and ginger in a large, deep, heatproof bowl. Put the chicken on top of the vegetables and pour in just enough water to cover it. Cover the top of the bowl tightly with kitchen foil.

place the bowl in a large saucepan of water, which should not come more than halfway up the sides of the bowl.

bring the water to the boil, then simmer for 1 hour, topping up with boiling water if necessary.

lift out the chicken. Place the sliced cabbage in the bottom of the bowl and sprinkle with the crumbled stock cubes.

replace the chicken. Tightly cover the bowl again with kitchen foil and simmer gently for 1 more hour.

arrange on a warmed platter, and garnish with coriander, if liked.

Serves 4–6
Preparation time: *10 minutes*
Cooking time: *2¼–2½ hours*

Cashew Chicken
with garlic, wine and ginger

A good example of how Chinese cooking orchestrates ingredients into perfect harmony, this is a popular classic dish.

375 g/12 oz boneless chicken
1 egg white, lightly beaten
4 tablespoons Chinese wine or dry sherry
2 teaspoons cornflour
3 tablespoons sunflower oil
4 spring onions, chopped
2 garlic cloves, chopped
1 x 2.5 cm/1 inch piece fresh root ginger, peeled and finely chopped
1 tablespoon light soy sauce
125 g/4 oz unsalted cashew nuts

cut the chicken into 1 cm/½ inch cubes. Mix together the egg white, half the wine or sherry and the cornflour.

place the chicken cubes in this mixture and toss until evenly coated.

heat the oil in a wok. Then add the spring onions, garlic and ginger, and stir-fry for 30 seconds.

add the chicken and cook for 2 minutes.

pour in the remaining wine or sherry and the soy sauce and stir well.

add the cashew nuts and cook for a further 30 seconds. Serve at once.

Serves 4
Preparation time: *5 minutes*
Cooking time: *3–4 minutes*

clipboard: Cashew nuts are widely used in Chinese cooking, and are highly prized for their sweet, rich flavour. As with other kinds of nuts, they are mostly used in chicken or in stir-fry vegetable dishes. Cashew nuts are very nutritious and are full of vitamins and minerals.

Ginger Chicken
with baby mushrooms

750 g/1½ lb chicken breasts, cut
into finger-sized pieces
1 teaspoon sugar
4 tablespoons sesame oil
1 x 10 cm/4 inch piece fresh root ginger, peeled and
finely sliced
75–100 ml/3–3½ fl oz water
125 g/4 oz button mushrooms
2 tablespoons brandy
2 teaspoons cornflour, blended with
3 tablespoons water
1 teaspoon light soy sauce
salt and pepper

sprinkle the chicken with the sugar and leave to stand for 20–30 minutes. Season with salt and pepper.

heat the oil and fry the ginger for 1 minute.

add the chicken pieces and cook for 3 minutes.

stir in the water and mushrooms. Cover and cook for a further 5 minutes, or until the chicken is tender.

add the brandy, cornflour mixture and soy sauce. Bring to the boil, stirring, until thickened. Serve at once.

Serves 4
Preparation time: *10 minutes, plus 20–30 minutes standing*
Cooking time: *10–15 minutes*

clipboard: Fresh ginger is required so often in Chinese cooking, it is worth keeping some on hand. It freezes very well — wrap it in cling film, or in a small freezer bag. You can use the amount you need, and return the rest to the freezer. Ginger can also be kept in the refrigerator in a tightly sealed jar of dry sherry. Ground ginger is not an acceptable substitute for the real thing.

Spicy Chicken
braised with coconut juice

2 tablespoons oil

1 x 1 kg/2 lb chicken, cut into serving pieces

1 tablespoon Chinese wine or dry sherry

2 tablespoons soy sauce

1 teaspoon salt

pinch of pepper

2 onions, cut into quarters

3 spring onions, chopped

3 garlic cloves, chopped

2 tablespoons curry paste

2 teaspoons curry powder

300 ml/½ pint water

3 medium potatoes, cut into 2.5 cm/1 inch pieces

2 medium carrots, cut into 2.5 cm/1 inch pieces

4 tablespoons coconut juice

2 tablespoons plain flour

2 teaspoons sugar

a few strips of green pepper, to garnish

heat 1 tablespoon of the oil in a pan. Add the chicken and stir-fry until lightly browned.

add the wine or sherry, soy sauce, salt and pepper. Stir-fry for 2 seconds, then add the onions. Stir-fry for 30 seconds, then transfer the mixture to a saucepan.

heat the remaining oil in the pan. Add the spring onions and garlic, and stir-fry for 1 second. Add the curry paste and curry powder.

stir-fry for 30 seconds, then stir in the water. Pour this sauce over the chicken and add the potatoes and carrots.

bring to the boil, cover and simmer for about 20 minutes, or until the chicken is tender.

combine the coconut juice with the flour and sugar and stir into the pan. Cook, stirring, until the sauce is thickened.

serve hot, garnished with strips of green pepper.

Serves 4
Preparation time: *15 minutes*
Cooking time: *30–40 minutes*

clipboard: This dish (and various other versions of it) is very popular in Singapore — so, though delicious, it is not a mainland Chinese recipe. A few drops of Tabasco or chilli sauce may be added with the curry paste to enhance the hot flavour, if liked.

Stir-fried Turkey
in a sweet and sour sauce

Turkey breast is becoming a popular choice for a quick, easy meal. Cooked with this exquisite sweet and sour sauce, it has a scrumptious taste.

Sauce

1½ tablespoons light soy sauce
1 heaped tablespoon tomato purée
2 teaspoons cornflour
300 ml/½ pint water
3 tablespoons unsweetened pineapple juice
2 tablespoons wine vinegar
1 heaped teaspoon brown sugar

Stir-fry

1 tablespoon sunflower oil
1 onion, finely chopped
1 turkey breast, skinned and cut into cubes
½ yellow or red pepper, cored, deseeded and sliced
3 mushrooms, sliced
spring onion, to garnish

make the sauce: place all the ingredients in a small pan and mix well.

bring to the boil, then simmer, stirring, until thickened. Keep warm.

heat the oil in a wok and stir-fry the onion for 2 minutes. Add the turkey and stir-fry for 2–3 minutes.

add the pepper and mushrooms and cook for 2–3 minutes.

transfer to a warmed serving dish and pour over the sauce. Garnish with spring onion and serve hot.

Serves 4
Preparation time: *6 minutes*
Cooking time: *6–10 minutes*

clipboard: This is a perfect recipe to use with the convenient packs of turkey breasts that are widely available in supermarkets. Turkey breast meat is healthily low in fat and calories, and has a more pronounced flavour than chicken. Turkey used to be a special occasion meat for Christmas and holidays — now it is an everyday ingredient.

Peking Duck

Arguably the most famous of all Chinese dishes, this was first served in 1864 at the Chuan Chu Te restaurant. It is now simply called the Peking Duck restaurant!

1 x 2–2.25 kg (4–4½ lb) oven-ready duck
2 tablespoons soy sauce
2 tablespoons dark brown sugar

Mandarin pancakes

1 quantity of dough for mandarin
pancakes (see page 238)

To serve

1 small cucumber, cut into 5 cm/2 inch
matchstick pieces
1 bunch spring onions, cut into 5 cm/2 inch
matchstick pieces
8 tablespoons hoisin sauce
spring onion tassel
(see page 62)

immerse the duck in a pan of boiling water for 2 minutes, then drain thoroughly. Hang up the duck to dry in a well ventilated room overnight. Mix together the soy sauce and sugar, and rub over the duck.

hang for 2 hours until the soy and sugar coating is completely dry. Place the duck on a rack in a roasting pan and cook in a preheated oven at 200°C/400°F/Gas Mark 6 for 1½ hours.

make the pancakes in the meantime (see method on page 238) and set them aside, keeping warm in a very low oven.

cut off all the crispy skin from the duck and arrange on a warmed serving dish. Garnish with cucumber.

remove all the meat and arrange on another warmed serving dish. Garnish with spring onion. Place the hoisin sauce in a small bowl. Garnish the pancakes with a spring onion tassel.

each guest prepares their own pancake. Spread a little hoisin sauce over a pancake. Cover with a piece of duck skin and meat, top with cucumber.

Serves 4–6
Preparation time: *1 hour, plus hanging overnight and for 2 hours the following day*
Cooking time: *1½ hours*
Oven temperature: *200°C/400°F/Gas Mark 6*

Eight-Treasure Duck *with ham, shiitake mushrooms and bamboo shoots*

1 x 2 kg/4 lb oven-ready duckling
2 tablespoons dark soy sauce
150 g/5 oz glutinous rice
200 ml/7 fl oz water
4–5 dried shiitake mushrooms
1 tablespoon dried shrimps
2 tablespoons sunflower oil
2 spring onions, finely chopped
2 slices fresh root ginger, chopped
125 g/4 oz bamboo shoots, cubed
125 g/4 oz cooked ham, cubed
1½ teaspoons salt
1 tablespoon light soy sauce
2 tablespoons Chinese wine or sherry

brush the duck skin with the soy sauce. Cook the rice in the water following the packet instructions. Prepare the mushrooms. Soak the shrimps in warm water for 20 minutes and drain.

heat the oil in a wok and stir-fry the spring onions and ginger for 30 seconds. Add the remaining ingredients, blend well and turn off the heat. Add the cooked rice and mix together all the ingredients.

pack this mixture into the duck cavity and close up the tail opening securely. Bake the duck on a wire rack in a pan in a preheated oven at 200°C/ 400°F/Gas Mark 6 for 30 minutes.

reduce the heat to 180°C/350°F/Gas Mark 4 for a further 45 minutes. Spoon the stuffing out of duck on to the centre of a dish. Cut the duck into neat pieces and arrange round the edge.

Serves 4–6
Preparation time: *35–40 minutes*
Cooking time: *1¼ hours*
Oven temperature: *200°C/ 400°F/Gas Mark 6,*
then *180°C/50°F/Gas Mark 4*

clipboard: The name of this dish refers to the number of favoured ingredients used for the stuffing. Eight is regarded as an auspicious number for complete balance and harmony.

Stir-fried Duck
with bamboo shoots and almonds

The Chinese simply adore the rich taste and luscious texture of duck. This stir-fry is a simple but succulent way of cooking it.

500 g/1 lb lean duck meat
2 slices root ginger, shredded
1 clove garlic, crushed
3 tablespoons sesame oil
3–4 dried Chinese mushrooms
4 spring onions, sliced
125 g/4 oz canned bamboo shoots, drained and sliced
3 tablespoons soy sauce
2 tablespoons Chinese wine or sherry
2 teaspoons cornflour
25 g/1 oz flaked almonds, toasted

cut the duck meat into small chunks and place them in a bowl with the ginger and garlic.

pour over 1 tablespoon of the oil and leave to marinate for 30 minutes.

soak the mushrooms in warm water for 15 minutes, if using. Squeeze dry, discard the hard stalks, then slice the mushroom caps.

heat the remaining oil in a wok or deep frying pan, add the spring onions and stir-fry for 30 seconds.

add the duck and cook for 2 minutes. Add the mushrooms, bamboo shoots, soy sauce and wine or sherry, and cook for 2 minutes.

blend the cornflour with 1 tablespoon water and stir into the pan. Cook for 1 minute, stirring, until thickened. Stir in the almonds and serve.

Serves 4–6
Preparation time: *15 minutes, plus 30 minutes marinating and 15 minutes soaking*
Cooking time: *6–7 minutes*

Braised Duck
with shiitake mushrooms

4 dried shiitake mushrooms

1 x 2 kg/4 lb duck, cut into individual portions

5 tablespoons light soy sauce

4 tablespoons sunflower oil

3 spring onions, chopped

4 slices fresh root ginger, peeled and chopped

3 star anise

1 teaspoon black peppercorns

2 teaspoons Chinese wine or dry sherry

125 g/4 oz canned bamboo shoots, drained and sliced

2 tablespoons cornflour

2 tablespoons water

star anise to garnish (optional)

soak the mushrooms in boiling water for 20 minutes. Drain and discard the stems.

rub the duck with a little soy sauce. Heat the oil in a wok or large frying pan and fry the duck until it is golden all over. Transfer the duck to a saucepan, add the spring onions, ginger, star anise, peppercorns, wine or sherry, remaining soy sauce and enough cold water to cover.

bring slowly to the boil, reduce the heat and simmer for 1½–2 hours. Add the mushrooms and bamboo shoots 20 minutes before the end of the cooking time.

mix the cornflour with the water and stir this mixture into the pan. Continue to cook until the sauce is thickened. Transfer to a warmed serving dish and serve hot, garnished with star anise, if liked.

Serves 4
Preparation time: *20 minutes, plus 20 minutes soaking*
Cooking time: *about 2½ hours*

clipboard: This dish can be started a day in advance. Simmer for 1½ hours, and leave to cool completely. Next day, skim off all excess fat, bring back to the boil and add the mushrooms and bamboo shoots. Simmer for 20 minutes and finish as above. Star anise is a Chinese spice with a distinctive liquorice flavour, shaped like a star with 8 points.

Barbecued Duck
with ginger and sesame seeds

4 boneless duck breasts, skin removed

Marinade
2 tablespoons brown sugar
1 teaspoon salt
4 tablespoons light soy sauce
1 tablespoon sesame oil
1 x 1 cm/½ inch piece fresh root ginger,
peeled and finely chopped
1 teaspoon sesame seeds

cut the duck breasts into 32 evenly sized pieces.

mix the marinade ingredients in a large bowl and add the duck.

stir, cover and marinate for 3–4 hours in a cool place or overnight in the refrigerator. Spoon the marinade over the duck several times, making sure that you coat the pieces evenly.

remove the duck with a slotted spoon and thread on to 8 bamboo skewers previously soaked in water, or 4 large metal skewers.

place the skewers on the grid of a moderately hot barbecue and cook the small skewers for 8–10 minutes, the larger ones for 10–12 minutes.

turn the skewers several times during cooking and baste with the remaining marinade.

serve the barbecued duck hot or cold, either on or off the skewers.

Serves 4
Preparation time: *20–25 minutes,*
plus 3–4 hours marinating
Cooking time: *8–12 minutes*

clipboard: You should be able to find pre-packed, ready-prepared duck breasts on sale at the poultry counter of larger supermarkets. They are excellent for stir-fries, or for barbecuing, as in this recipe.

Roast Pigeons *in a honey, soy and garlic glaze*

4 oven-ready pigeons
175 ml/6 fl oz rice alcohol or vodka

Marinade
5 tablespoons sunflower oil
3 garlic cloves, crushed
½ onion, finely chopped
2 tablespoons light soy sauce
2 tablespoons honey or golden syrup
⅓ teaspoon 5-spice powder
pinch of freshly ground black pepper
6 tablespoons water

Lemon dip
2 lemons, cut in quarters
2 teaspoons salt
freshly ground black pepper

prepare the pigeons by rubbing them inside and out with rice alcohol or vodka. Place on a wire rack and set aside to dry.

combine all the ingredients for the marinade.

paint the pigeons with this mixture inside and out, and leave to dry for 1 hour, either on a rack in a cool, well-ventilated room or preferably hanging by their necks.

brush the pigeons with the remaining marinade and roast on a rack in a pan in a preheated oven at 230°C/450°F/Gas Mark 8 for 20 minutes.

strip the flesh from the cooked pigeons and arrange on a warmed plate.

divide the lemon wedges among 4 dinner plates and add ½ teaspoon salt and a pinch of pepper to each.

make the dip: Each person makes their own dip by mixing the salt and pepper and moistening the mixture with a squeeze of lemon juice.

Serves 4
Preparation time: *30 minutes, plus 1 hour standing*
Cooking time: *20 minutes*
Oven temperature: *230°C/450°F/Gas Mark 8*

clipboard: Pigeons are widely used in Chinese cooking, usually braised or deep-fried. The secret of success is that the pigeons are marinated first to tenderize the flesh and to keep it from drying out.

Special equipment

Wok

Garlic press

Colander

Wok

The wok is the most essential item in Chinese cooking, and many other kitchen tools are designed to work in conjunction with it. The wok is both hard working and versatile; the round-bottomed design with sloping sides ensures that food can be deep-fried or stir-fried quickly, whilst using the minimum of oil. The wok's surface is also a good heat conductor. With a few basic accessories food can be steamed, braised or smoked as well as stir-fried. Woks usually come complete with a steaming rack, and with a domed lid for steaming and braising. In addition, you will need a stand with sloping sides to place over the cooker hob. This holds the wok in place at the heat source. Before using a wok for the first time it should be thoroughly cleaned with detergent. Thereafter, simply wash it in hot water.

Garlic press

A garlic press is a very useful kitchen tool. The garlic is forced through a series of very small holes, allowing the oils to escape, and releasing the full flavour of the garlic. It protects the skin from the pungent aroma of the oil, and can also be used to extract juice from ginger.

Colander

The colander is used for separating liquids and solids and for draining and rinsing

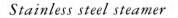

Stainless steel steamer

Sieve

Measuring spoon

food. Although colanders come in many shapes and sizes they are basically a container punched through with holes. They are usually made of plastic or stainless steel. The latter is much more practical as it is heat resistant, dishwasher-proof and hard wearing.

Sieve

A sieve has a rigid frame and a mesh dome in variations from fine to coarse. It can be used for separating solids from liquids, solids from solids, and also for refining ingredients. The mesh should be stainless steel to prevent rust.

Measuring spoon

Measuring spoons come in sets with a tablespoon, a teaspoon, half teaspoon, and a quarter teaspoon. They are available in aluminium, plastic or stainless steel and are used for measuring both dry and liquid ingredients. When measuring liquids the spoons are filled to the top. Level off dry ingredients unless a rounded measure is required.

Stainless steel steamer

Essentially the stainless steel steamer has exactly the same function as the bamboo steamer, though the latter often has several layers of steamers in use at any one time. It is certainly more modern and more practical to maintain and clean, and also lasts a lot longer. It is excellent for maintaining the texture and the flavour of the finished dish.

Rice and Noodles

Egg Noodles
in yellow bean and chilli sauce

Egg noodles are mainly used in northern China. They are just like pasta, which makes a good substitute. Marco Polo is reputed to have brought the recipe for making them home to Italy after his travels in China.

375 g/12 oz egg noodles or spaghettini
3 tablespoons yellow bean paste
2 teaspoons chilli sauce
1 garlic clove, crushed
3 tablespoons oil
2 green peppers, cored and deseeded
1 medium onion, thinly sliced
150 g/5 oz beansprouts
salt

cook the noodles or spaghettini in boiling, salted water for 5 minutes, or until it is just firm to the bite (*al dente*). Drain.

mix together the yellow bean paste, chilli sauce and garlic.

heat the oil in a wok or large frying pan on a high heat. Put in the peppers, onion and beansprouts and stir-fry for 2 minutes.

add the noodles and stir in the sauce mixture.

heat through and transfer to a warmed serving dish.

Serves 4
Preparation time: *10 minutes*
Cooking time: *10 minutes*

clipboard: Bean sauces are popular flavourings in Chinese cooking — yellow bean sauce is milder than black bean sauce. It is made from salted soya beans, garlic, soy sauce, vinegar, sugar, and seasoning.

Fresh Noodles
with sesame paste sauce

Fresh noodles are available at Chinese food stores, and are particularly delicious. Here they are flavoured with an aromatic sesame sauce in a hot stock.

500 g/1 lb fresh noodles
900 ml/1½ pints Chicken Stock (see page 11)

Sauce

2 tablespoons sesame seed paste
4 tablespoons water
4 tablespoons spring onions, chopped
1 teaspoon soy sauce
2 teaspoons red wine vinegar
2 teaspoons chilli oil
1 teaspoon salt

cook the noodles in plenty of boiling, salted water until just tender. Bring the stock to the boil in another pan.

make the sauce: mix the sesame seed paste with the water, then add the remaining ingredients.

when the noodles are cooked, drain well. Divide the boiling stock between four individual soup bowls.

add the cooked noodles and top with the sauce. Each person tosses the contents of his bowl before eating.

Serves 4–6
Preparation time: *10 minutes*
Cooking time: *10–15 minutes*

clipboard: Sesame paste is a favourite ingredient in Chinese sauces. It is quite similar to peanut butter, and has a very rich and aromatic flavour. Chilli oil is available at Chinese food stores — you only need a small bottle as it must be used very sparingly.

Singapore Noodles

This is one of many versions of the tasty noodle dish sold by Singapore street hawkers. You can create your own variations, of course, but this one makes a really good late supper dish.

2 nests dry noodles
575 ml/18 fl oz water
125 g/4 oz lean pork, cut into 5 cm/2 inch strips
75 g/3 oz uncooked prawns, shelled
75 g/3 oz squid, cleaned and sliced
4 tablespoons sunflower oil
2 garlic cloves, crushed
75 g/3 oz beansprouts
1 tablespoon light soy sauce
1 tablespoon dark soy sauce
½ teaspoon freshly ground black pepper
1 bunch fresh chives, chopped
2 eggs

boil the noodles in plenty of water for 2 minutes. Drain.

bring the measured water to the boil in a pan and cook the pork, prawns and squid together for 5 minutes. Drain and reserve the liquid.

heat the oil in a wok or frying pan and fry the garlic until golden. Add the beansprouts and noodles, increase the heat, and stir-fry for 2 minutes.

add the pork, prawns and squid, the soy sauces, pepper and chives and stir-fry for 1 minute more.

push the mixture to one side of the pan and crack in the eggs. Cook for 1 minute and add the reserved liquid.

bring to the boil and cook for 2 minutes, stirring well. Transfer to a warmed serving dish and serve at once.

Serves 4
Preparation time: *15 minutes*
Cooking time: *14–18 minutes*

clipboard: Dried rice-stick noodles are sold in packets at supermarkets and Chinese food stores. These convenient packages resemble little nests, so they are easy to recognise.

Crispy Fried Noodles *with spinach, chicken and prawns*

3 celery sticks
125 g/4 oz spinach
500 g/1 lb egg noodles or fettucine
1 tablespoon oil
1 clove garlic, sliced
1 piece root ginger, finely chopped
3 spring onions, chopped
125 g/4 oz lean pork, sliced
125 g/4 oz boned chicken breast, shredded
1 tablespoon soy sauce
1 tablespoon Chinese wine or dry sherry
50 g/2 oz frozen peeled prawns, thawed

slice the celery sticks diagonally and shred the spinach.

cook the noodles or fettucine in boiling, salted, water according to the packet instructions, until just tender. Do not overcook.

drain and rinse with cold water.

heat the oil in a wok or deep frying pan, add the garlic, ginger and spring onions and fry for 1 minute.

add the pork and chicken and stir-fry for 2 minutes. Add the noodles, soy sauce, wine or sherry and prawns, and cook for 3 minutes.

pile on to a warmed serving dish and serve immediately.

Serves 4–6
Preparation time: *15 minutes*
Cooking time: *15–20 minutes*

clipboard: Chinese noodles are satisfyingly versatile in that they can be boiled and then stir-fried. When you use this method, do make sure that they are *barely* tender before stir-frying, as over-cooking spoils their texture and makes them slightly sticky.

Tossed Noodles
with pork and vegetables

This is the sort of savoury, aromatic noodle dish that tranfers well to a modern, hectic life-style. It is full of interesting flavours, cooked in minutes, and makes a satisfying supper.

2 tablespoons oil

2 green chillies, deseeded, thinly sliced

1 clove garlic, thinly sliced

375 g/12 oz minced pork

2 carrots, cut into matchstick lengths

3 celery sticks, cut into matchstick lengths

½ cucumber, cut into matchstick lengths

4 spring onions, sliced

1 small green pepper, cored, deseeded and sliced

1 tablespoon soy sauce

2 tablespoons sweet red bean paste

1 tablespoon Chinese wine or dry sherry

375 g/12 oz noodles or spaghettini, cooked

heat the oil in a wok or deep frying pan, add the chillies and garlic and fry quickly for about 30 seconds.

add the pork and cook for 2 minutes. Increase the heat, add the vegetables and cook for 1 minute.

stir in the soy sauce, bean paste, wine or sherry and noodles or spaghettini. Stir well to mix and heat through.

pile on to a warmed serving dish and serve immediately.

Serves 4–6
Preparation time: *10 minutes*
Cooking time: *5 minutes*

Transparent Noodles *with pork and black bean paste*

125 g/4 oz transparent noodles
250 g/8 oz lean minced pork
1 teaspoon cornflour
2 tablespoons light soy sauce
1 tablespoon hot black bean paste
125 ml/4 fl oz Chicken Stock (see page 11) or water
4 tablespoons sunflower oil
4 spring onions, finely chopped
1 fresh green chilli, deseeded and finely chopped

soak the noodles in warm water for 10 minutes. Drain. Mix the pork with the cornflour and soy sauce.

combine the bean paste with the stock or water.

heat the oil over high heat in a wok or large frying pan. Add the pork and stir-fry for about 2 minutes until it has browned.

stir in the noodles, spring onions, chilli and finally, the bean paste mixture.

bring to the boil and stir for about 1 minute, until all the moisture has evaporated.

transfer to a warmed serving dish and serve immediately.

Serves 4
Preparation time: *10 minutes, plus 10 minutes soaking*
Cooking time: *4–5 minutes*

clipboard: Transparent noodles, also known as beanthread or cellophane noodles, are used here to add bulk to a stir-fry, which makes a delicious and filling all-in-one dish.

Chow Mein

*Literally translated, this means "stir-fried noodles"
and was created by Chinese immigrants in America.
It is also versatile, so you can use whatever
ingredients you have available!*

500 g/1 lb egg noodles or spaghettini
4 tablespoons vegetable oil
1 medium onion, peeled and thinly sliced
125 g/4 oz cooked meat (pork, chicken or ham)
cut into thin shreds
125 g/4 oz mangetout, or French beans
125 g/4 oz fresh beansprouts
1 teaspoon salt
2–3 spring onions, thinly shredded
2 tablespoons light soy sauce
1 tablespoon sesame seed oil or chilli sauce, to finish
salt for boiling

cook the noodles or spaghettini in a large saucepan of boiling, salted water according to packet instructions.

drain and rinse under cold running water until cool, and set aside.

heat about 3 tablespoons of the oil in a hot wok, add the onion, meat, mangetout or beans and the beansprouts, and stir-fry for about 1 minute.

add 1 teaspoon salt and stir a few times more, then remove from the wok with a perforated spoon and keep hot.

heat the remaining oil in the wok and add the spring onions and the noodles, with about half of the meat and vegetable mixture.

mix with the soy sauce, then stir-fry for 1–2 minutes, or until completely heated through.

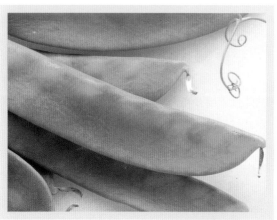

transfer the mixture from the wok to a warmed, large serving dish, then pour the remaining meat and vegetable mixture on top as a dressing.

sprinkle with the sesame seed oil or chilli sauce (or both if preferred). Serve immediately.

Serves 4
Preparation time: *15 minutes*
Cooking time: *15–18 minutes*

Chicken Chop Suey *with garlic*

2 tablespoons oil
5 spring onions, chopped
2.5 cm/1 inch piece root ginger, peeled and chopped
2 garlic cloves, crushed
175 g/6 oz chicken breast, skinned
and cut into thin strips
1 tablespoon tomato purée
2 tablespoons Chinese wine or dry sherry
2 tablespoons soy sauce
1 teaspoon sugar
8 tablespoons water
300 g/10 oz beansprouts
3 eggs, beaten with 2 tablespoons water

heat 1 tablespoon of the oil, add the spring onions and ginger, and stir-fry for 1 minute.

add the garlic and chicken, and stir-fry for 2 minutes. Lower the heat, add the tomato purée, wine or sherry, soy sauce, sugar and 5 tablespoons of the water.

heat through gently, then transfer to a warmed serving dish.

heat 2 teaspoons of the oil in the pan, add the beansprouts and remaining water, and stir-fry for 3 minutes.

add to the serving dish and keep warm.

wipe out the pan and heat the remaining oil. Pour in the beaten eggs and cook until set and crisp.

place on top of the beansprout mixture and serve at once.

Serves 4
Preparation time: *8 minutes*
Cooking time: *8–10 minutes*

clipboard: The term Chop Suey comes from the Chinese word zasui which means "mixed bits". Small portions of meat, fish and vegetables can be thrown in, so you can use up left-overs. Do try and use at least one fresh vegetable, however, to give a crisp, fresh flavour to the dish.

Fried Rice
with ham and beansprouts

If you have some leftover rice, it is ideal to use in this quick, tasty recipe. You can prepare all the ingredients in advance, and stir-fry just before serving.

2 tablespoons sunflower oil
2 spring onions, finely chopped
I garlic clove, crushed
375 g/12 oz long-grain rice, cooked
175 g/6 oz cooked ham, diced
2 tablespoons light soy sauce
2 eggs
250 g/8 oz beansprouts, rinsed and drained
salt and pepper

heat the oil in a wok or pan over moderate heat and stir-fry the spring onions and garlic for 2 minutes.

add the cooked rice next and stir well. Cook gently, stirring continously, as the rice heats through.

stir in the ham and soy sauce. Beat the eggs thoroughly, with salt and pepper to taste.

pour into the rice mixture in a thin stream, stirring all the time.

add the beansprouts and continue cooking, stirring until all the ingredients are hot and the eggs are set. Serve at once.

Serves 4
Preparation time: *15 minutes*
Cooking time: *8–10 minutes*

clipboard: You don't need a special variety of ham for this recipe — ordinary boiled ham is easy to obtain, and is perfectly suitable.

Spicy Fried Rice
with red chillies

Chilli pepper fans will adore this dish, but it also tastes very good made with paprika instead, and the colour will be just as attractive.

375 g/12 oz long-grain rice
450 ml/¾ pint water
2 tablespoons sunflower oil
4 shallots or 1 onion, thinly sliced
2 fresh red chillies, deseeded and thinly sliced
50 g/2 oz chopped pork, beef or bacon
1 tablespoon light soy sauce
1 teaspoon tomato purée
salt

To garnish
a few slices of fried onion
1 plain omelette, made with 1 egg, cut into strips
a few fresh coriander leaves
a few cucumber slices

cook the rice (see Plain Boiled Rice page 132) and keep hot.

heat the oil in a wok or frying pan, add the shallots and chillies and fry for 1–3 minutes.

add the meat or bacon and fry for 3 minutes, stirring constantly.

add the rice, soy sauce and tomato purée and stir-fry for 5–8 minutes, then season with salt to taste.

transfer to a warmed serving dish and garnish with the onion, omelette, coriander and cucumber. Serve at once.

Serves 4
Preparation time: *15 minutes*
Cooking time: *about 25–30 minutes*

clipboard: Fresh chillies are easily available at supermarkets and grocers. The seeds are the hottest part. wear rubber gloves to remove them. Slit the chilli lengthways down the centre, hold it under a cold tap, and rub off the seeds. When handling chillies, don't put your fingers near your eyes, as the pungent juices will irritate and sting them.

Cantonese Rice

with prawns, meat and fresh mixed vegetables

250 g/8 oz long-grain rice, cooked
125 g/4 oz prawns
2 teaspoons salt
1 egg white, lightly beaten
2 tablespoons cornflour
1 pig's kidney, halved and trimmed
1 chicken liver, finely sliced
125 g/4 oz green beans, halved
3 tablespoons sunflower oil
2 spring onions, cut into short lengths
125 g/4 oz roast pork, finely sliced
125 g/4 oz white fish fillet, cubed
1 teaspoon sugar
2 tablespoons light soy sauce
4 tablespoons Chicken stock (see page 11)

cook the rice (see Plain Boiled Rice page 132) and keep hot.

put the prawns in a bowl with a pinch of salt, the egg white and 1 tablespoon of cornflour and toss to coat.

score the surface of each kidney half in a crisscross pattern, then cut each half into 6–8 pieces.

blanch the prawns, kidney, liver and green beans in boiling water for 10–15 seconds, and drain.

heat the oil in a wok or pan and stir-fry the spring onions briefly.

add all the meats, fish and vegetables, with salt to taste, the sugar and soy sauce. Stir-fry for 1 minute.

combine the remaining cornflour with the stock and add to the wok, stirring. Serve on a bed of rice.

Serves 4
Preparation time: *30 minutes*
Cooking time: *30–35 minutes*

Special Rice

wrapped in lotus leaves

This dish lives up to its exotic name as it is delicately perfumed by the lotus leaf wrapping.

175 g/6 oz long-grain rice, cooked
1 tablespoon sunflower oil
1 garlic clove, crushed
3 spring onions, chopped
125 g/4 oz button mushrooms, sliced
50 g/2 oz cooked ham, diced
125 g/4 oz cooked chicken, diced
1 tablespoon green peas
50 g/2 oz canned bamboo shoots, drained and chopped
2 tablespoons light soy sauce
2 tablespoons Chinese wine or dry sherry
8 lotus leaves

cook the rice (see Plain Boiled Rice page 132) and keep hot. Soak the lotus leaves in warm water for 30 minutes. Drain thoroughly.

heat the oil in a wok or deep frying pan, add the garlic and spring onions and stir-fry for 1 minute.

add the remaining ingredients, except the lotus leaves, and continue cooking for 2 minutes. Cut each lotus leaf into 2 or 3 pieces and divide the mixture evenly among them.

fold the leaf sections to enclose the filling like a parcel, and secure with string. Place in a steamer and steam vigorously for 15–20 minutes.

pile the parcels on to a warmed serving dish and serve immediately so everyone can open their own parcels.

Serves 4–6
Preparation time: *20 minutes, plus 30 minutes soaking*
Cooking time: *30–35 minutes*

clipboard: Dried lotus leaves are used for wrapping food, but when fresh they can add a distinct flavour to dishes. If you can't buy them, use one vine leaf for each parcel instead.

Plain Boiled Rice

In China, rice is regarded as being almost sacred. It is so important that it is considered very bad luck to tip over or break a rice bowl.

250 g/8 oz medium grain rice
600 ml/1 pint cold water
1 teaspoon of salt

put the rice, water and salt into a saucepan. Set on a moderate heat and bring to the boil.

stir, then cover and simmer for 15 minutes or until all the water has been absorbed.

tip the rice into a colander or large sieve. Run through with cold water to stop the cooking process.

run through with hot water to clear any stickiness.

turn the rice on to a wide, flat dish and leave in a warm place for about 5 minutes to dry.

fluff it with a fork twice during that time to separate the grains and ensure even drying.

Serves 4
Preparation time: *5 minutes, plus 5 minutes standing*
Cooking time: *15–20 minutes*

clipboard: Medium- and short-grain rice are generally preferred in Chinese cooking, as the cooked grains are so much easier to pick up with chopsticks. Although easy-cook or 'converted' rice is widely available, and will give the requisite fluffy, non-sticky texture, purists do not recommend it, as they believe it does not taste as good.

Steamed Rice

If you do not have a steamer, you may like to consider the pretty bamboo basket steamers that are on sale at Chinese food stores. They are not very expensive, and you can use them to serve food if you like.

250 g/8 oz medium grain rice
1 teaspoon of salt

bring a large pan of salted water to the boil. Scatter in the rice, cover and cook on a low heat for 5 minutes. Drain, run through with hot water and drain again.

put the rice into a bamboo steamer or a vegetable steamer.

set the steamer over boiling water, taking care that the water does not bubble up through the rice.

use the handle of a wooden spoon to make several holes through the rice for the steam to circulate.

cover the pan and steam the rice for 45 minutes.

turn the rice on to a wide, flat dish and leave in a warm place for about 5 minutes to dry.

fluff it with a fork twice during that time to separate the grains and ensure even drying.

Serves 4
Preparation time: *5 minutes*
Cooking time: *50 minutes*

Meat

Pork Spareribs
with spicy chilli sauce

Tender, succulent spareribs have always been prized by Chinese cooks. Cook them in this sizzling, spicy sauce for a mouthwatering treat.

Chilli sauce

4 tablespoons clear honey

4 tablespoons wine vinegar

2 tablespoons light soy sauce

2 tablespoons Chinese wine or dry sherry

1 x 150 g/5 oz can tomato purée

1 teaspoon chilli powder

2 garlic cloves, crushed

1 kg/2 lb lean pork spareribs, cut into 5 cm/2 inch pieces

2 tablespoons sunflower oil

2 dried red chillies, deseeded and cut into small rings

1 x 2.5 cm/1 inch piece fresh root ginger, peeled and finely chopped

1 garlic clove, thinly sliced

1 dried red chilli, deseeded and cut into small rings, to garnish (optional)

salt

make the chilli sauce: mix all the ingredients together and set aside.

sprinkle the spareribs with salt.

heat the oil in a wok and quickly fry the red chillies to flavour it.

remove the chillies with a slotted spoon and discard them. Next, add the chopped ginger and garlic to the wok and stir-fry over moderate heat for 30 seconds.

add the spareribs and stir-fry for 5 minutes, until golden brown. Reduce the heat and cook gently for 10 minutes.

add the sauce to the wok, cover and simmer gently for 25–30 minutes. Serve hot, garnished with the chilli rings, if liked.

Serves 4–6
Preparation time: *15 minutes*
Cooking time: *40–45 minutes*

clipboard: Provide several small bowls of warm water and plenty of paper napkins whenever you are serving spareribs or other food that is usually eaten with the fingers.

Twice-Cooked Pork *with hot bean sauce*

375 g/12 oz pork belly in one piece
125 g/4 oz bamboo shoots
125 g/4 oz celery sticks
3 tablespoons sunflower oil
2 spring onions, chopped
1 garlic clove, chopped
2 tablespoons Chinese wine or dry sherry
1 tablespoon light soy sauce
1 tablespoon chilli bean paste

place the whole piece of pork in a pan of boiling water and cook for 25–30 minutes. Remove and leave to cool.

slice the meat thinly, cutting across the grain, into pieces not much larger than a postage stamp.

cut the bamboo shoots and celery into 5 cm/2 inch chunks.

heat the oil in a wok or deep frying pan until smoking.

add the spring onions and garlic to flavour the oil, then add the vegetables and stir-fry briefly.

add the pork, then the wine or sherry, soy sauce and chilli bean paste. Stir-fry for 2 minutes.

transfer to a warmed dish and serve immediately with noodles.

Serves 3–4
Preparation time: *15 minutes*
Cooking time: *35–40 minutes*

clipboard: This recipe combines two cooking methods in a technique known as 'cross-cooking'. This involves boiling and then stir-frying, to ensure full flavour and a crisp texture.

Stir-fried Pork and Aubergine

175 g/6 oz boned lean pork, shredded
2 spring onions, finely chopped
1 slice of fresh root ginger, peeled and finely chopped
1 garlic clove, peeled and finely chopped
1 tablespoon soy sauce
1 teaspoon Chinese wine or or dry sherry
1½ teaspoons cornflour
600 ml/1 pint vegetable oil for deep-frying
250 g/8 oz aubergine, cut into
diamond-shaped chunks
1 tablespoon chilli sauce
3–4 tablespoons Chicken Stock
(see page 11) or water
chopped spring onion, to garnish

put the pork in a bowl with the spring onions, ginger, garlic, soy sauce, wine or sherry and cornflour.

mix well, then leave to marinate for about 20 minutes.

heat the oil in a wok or deep-fat fryer to 180°C/350°F or until a cube of day-old bread browns in 45 seconds.

lower the heat, add the aubergine and deep-fry for about 1½ minutes.

remove from the pan with a slotted spoon and drain.

pour off all but 1 tablespoon of oil from the pan, then add the pork and stir-fry for about 1 minute.

add the aubergine and chilli sauce and cook for about 1½ minutes, then moisten with the stock or water.

simmer until the liquid has almost completely evaporated. Serve hot, with plain boiled rice, garnished with chopped spring onions.

Serves 3–4
Preparation time: *10 minutes,
plus 20 minutes marinating*
Cooking time: *10–15 minutes*

Cantonese Pork
in sweet and sour sauce

The extremes of sweet and sour in this sauce are meant to represent Yin and Yang in perfect harmony.

500 g/1 lb pork fillet, cut into 2.5 cm/1 inch cubes
1 teaspoon salt
pinch of pepper
½ teaspoon five-spice powder
2 tablespoons Chinese wine or dry sherry
1 egg
3 tablespoons cornflour
vegetable oil for deep-frying
2 tablespoons oil
1 garlic clove, crushed
1 onion, roughly chopped
1–2 green peppers, cored, deseeded and diced
1 x 250 g/8 oz can pineapple chunks, with juice
3 tablespoons wine vinegar
50 g/2 oz sugar
4 tablespoons tomato ketchup

fill the saucepan with water and bring to the boil. Add the pork and boil until it changes colour.

drain the pork, cool and pat dry with absorbent kitchen paper.

mix together the salt, pepper, five-spice powder, wine or sherry, egg and cornflour. Add the pork and turn to coat well.

heat the oil to 180°C/350°F or until a cube of day-old bread browns in 45 seconds. Deep-fry the pork until brown. Drain thoroughly on absorbent kitchen paper.

heat the 2 tablespoons of oil in a pan. Add the garlic and fry until brown. Add the onion and green pepper, and stir-fry for 1 minute. Stir in the pineapple juice with the vinegar, sugar and tomato ketchup.

cook, stirring, until thickened. Add the pineapple and stir until heated through. Serve hot, garnished with the pineapple chunks.

Serves 4–6
Preparation time: *10 minutes*
Cooking time: *20–30 minutes*

clipboard: Five-spice powder is a Chinese mixture of five spices — anise pepper, star anise, cinnamon, cloves and fennel seeds. It is strong and pungent and should be used sparingly.

Pork Slices
in honey and ginger sauce

Soaked and glazed in a luscious aromatic marinade, then quickly roasted, an economical cut of pork is cooked to perfection.

Marinade

2 tablespoons soy sauce

2 tablespoons Chinese wine or dry sherry

2 teaspoons sesame seed oil

1 teaspoon salt

2 teaspoons ginger juice (see page 24)

2 tablespoons clear honey or golden syrup

50 g/2 oz sugar

1–2 cloves garlic, crushed

1kg/3 lb pork shoulder, cut into 5 x 5 x 10cm/2 x 2 x 8 inch pieces

mix together the marinade ingredients in a large dish.

add the pork and leave to marinate for at least 6 hours in the refrigerator, turning the meat occasionally.

place the pieces of pork on a wire rack in a roasting pan. Roast in a preheated moderate oven at 180°C/350°F/Gas Mark 4 for 40–45 minutes or until tender, basting with the pan juices frequently.

cut into serving pieces and arrange on a plate. Serve hot or cold.

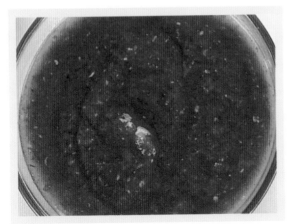

Serves 6
Preparation time: *10 minutes, plus 6 hours marinating*
Cooking time: *40–45 minutes*
Oven temperature: *180°C/350°F/Gas Mark 4*

clipboard: Pork shoulder is a good quality economical joint with an excellent flavour. Ask your butcher to chop it into evenly-sized pieces as specified in the ingredients, as this is difficult to do at home.

Fried Pork

with baby corn and mangetout

The luscious combination of flavours and textures in this quickly cooked dish is typical of Chinese cooking at its simplest and best.

1 tablespoon Chinese wine or dry sherry
1 tablespoon light soy sauce
1½ teaspoons cornflour
500 g/1 lb pork fillet, sliced as thinly as possible
1 tablespoon sunflower oil
500 g/1 lb baby corn
1 teaspoon salt
50 g/2 oz mangetout
1 x 475 g/15 oz can straw mushrooms, drained
2 teaspoons sugar
2 teaspoons water

mix the wine or sherry and soy sauce with 1 teaspoon of the cornflour. Add the pork and toss to coat well.

heat the oil in a wok or frying pan and stir-fry the pork until it is lightly browned.

add the baby corn and salt, and stir-fry for 30 seconds. Add the mangetout and mushrooms, and stir-fry for 1 minute.

sprinkle in the sugar.

mix the remaining cornflour with the water to make a thin paste and add this to the wok, stirring until the sauce is thickened.

transfer to a warmed serving dish and serve hot.

Serves 4
Preparation time: *5 minutes*
Cooking time: *5–8 minutes*

clipboard: Baby sweetcorn are usually available all year round at supermarkets. They are also available in cans. If you use the canned variety, they need half the cooking time of fresh sweetcorn.

Red-cooked Pork
with chestnuts

1.5–2 kg/3–4 lb belly pork
1½ teaspoons sugar
125 ml/4 fl oz water
5½ tablespoons soy sauce
250 g/8 oz chestnuts
5 tablespoons Chinese wine or dry sherry

cut the pork through the skin, lean, and fat, into 4 cm/1½ inch pieces. Combine the sugar, water and 4½ tablespoons of the soy sauce.

put the pork pieces in a flameproof casserole and pour over just enough boiling water to cover.

simmer for 15 minutes, then drain off all the water. Pour in the soy sauce mixture. Stir the pork pieces in the sauce until well coated.

transfer to a preheated cool oven at 150°C/300°F/Gas Mark 2 and cook for 1 hour, stirring twice.

meanwhile, cook the chestnuts in boiling water for 30 minutes. Drain, then remove the shells and skin.

add the chestnuts to the pork with the wine or sherry and the remaining soy sauce. Stir well and return to the oven for a further 1 hour.

serve hot, on cooked shredded cabbage, if liked.

Serves 10
Preparation time: *20 minutes*
Cooking time: *2¼–3hours*
Oven temperature: *150°C/300°F/Gas Mark 2*

clipboard: Red-cooking is a unique Chinese style of cooking. The food is stewed in a mixture of soy sauce, water and sugar, with wine and flavourings. It takes on an "auspicious" red colour during cooking.

Braised Pork
with pumpkin and ginger

375 g/12 oz lean pork
4 tablespoons soy sauce
3 tablespoons dry sherry
500 g/1 lb pumpkin flesh
4 spring onions
2 tablespoons oil
1 piece root ginger, shredded
2 cloves garlic, sliced

To garnish

carrot flowers
spring onion sliced
coriander leaves

cut the pork into 1 cm/½ inch slices. Put the soy sauce and sherry in a bowl and add the pork.

mix well and leave to marinate for 20 minutes.

cut the pumpkin flesh into 2.5 cm/1 inch cubes.

slice each spring onion into 3 pieces. Heat the oil in a wok or frying pan, add the pumpkin and fry quickly until browned.

add the spring onions, ginger and garlic, and cook for 1 minute.

add the pork and marinade and cook for 12–15 minutes, until the pork and pumpkin are tender.

spoon the mixture on to a warmed serving dish, garnish with carrot flowers, spring onion slices and coriander. Serve immediately.

Serves 4–6
Preparation time: *15 minutes, plus 20 minutes marinating*
Cooking time: *about 20 minutes*

clipboard: To make carrot flowers: peel a whole carrot and trim the top and bottom. Cut out 6 "v"-shaped strips lengthways down the sides of the carrot. Slice the carrot across into narrow rings, which will look just like little flowers.

Braised Lamb
with soy and mandarin sauce

4 mandarin oranges or 2 large oranges
1 tablespoon oil
4 leg of lamb steaks
6 spring onions, shredded
1 tablespoon Chinese wine or sherry
1 tablespoon light soy sauce
150 ml/¼ pint Chicken Stock (see page 11)
25 g/1 oz brown sugar
salt (optional) and freshly ground black pepper

pare the rind from the oranges thinly with a potato peeler. Squeeze the juice from the oranges and reserve.

shred the rind finely, blanch in boiling water for 5 minutes and drain.

heat the oil in the wok. Add the lamb and fry until browned on both sides. Remove from the wok.

add the onions to the wok and fry for 3 minutes. Place the lamb on top of the onions.

add the juice squeezed from the oranges, orange rind shreds, the wine or sherry, soy sauce, chicken stock, brown sugar, and pepper.

cover with the lid and braise over a low heat for 40 minutes or until the lamb is tender.

check the seasoning during cooking, and add salt to taste if necessary.

serve on a bed of plain boiled rice, topped with the orange rind shreds.

Serves 4
Preparation time: *15 minutes*
Cooking time: *55 minutes*

clipboard: Salt may be added to this recipe if liked — however do remember that the soy sauce is salty, and you should always check the taste first before adding any salt.

Tung-Po Lamb
stir-fry with mixed vegetables

*This is a light variation of a regional dish
named after Tung Po, the famous Tang dynasty poet*

2 tablespoons sunflower oil
750 g/1½ lb very lean lamb, thinly sliced
250 g/8 oz carrots, sliced diagonally
4 celery sticks, sliced diagonally
3 tablespoons light soy sauce
4 tablespoons Chinese wine or dry sherry
2 leeks, sliced
4 garlic cloves, thinly sliced
4 spring onions, cut into 2.5 cm/1 inch lengths
1 x 5 cm/2 inch piece fresh root ginger,
peeled and shredded
1 teaspoon lightly crushed black peppercorns
2 teaspoons brown sugar
flat-leaf parsley, to garnish

heat the oil in a wok or deep frying pan, add the lamb and cook until it is brown on all sides.

reduce the heat, add the carrots and celery and stir-fry for 2 minutes.

stir in the soy sauce and wine or sherry. Cover and cook for 15 minutes, until the vegetables are tender.

add the leeks, garlic, spring onions and ginger and cook for 1 minute.

add the peppercorns and sugar, and heat through, stirring, until the sugar dissolves. Garnish with flat-leaf parsley and serve at once.

Serves 4–6
Preparation time: *15 minutes*
Cooking time: *20–25 minutes*

clipboard: The ideal cut of lamb for stir-frying is lamb fillet, the strip of tender boneless meat from the neck. If this is unavailable, use lean, fillet end of leg of lamb, from which all the fat has been removed.

Shredded Lamb

stir-fried with noodles and spring onions

1 egg, beaten

1 tablespoon cornflour

1½ tablespoons water

250 g/8 oz lean lamb, shredded

3 tablespoons sunflower oil

2 tablespoons soy sauce

4–5 spring onions, cut into 5 cm/2 inch pieces

300 ml/½ pint Chicken Stock (see page 11)

125 g/4 oz cellophane noodles, soaked in hot water for 5 minutes and drained

1 tablespoon sesame seed oil

2 tablespoons Chinese wine or dry sherry

beat the egg with the cornflour and water.

add the lamb and turn it in the mixture to coat it.

heat the oil in a pan over high heat.

add the lamb and stir-fry for 1 minute. Sprinkle in the soy sauce and spring onions and stir-fry for 1 minute.

add the stock and noodles and bring to the boil, stirring. Simmer gently for 5 minutes.

sprinkle with the sesame seed oil and wine or sherry. Simmer for a further 1 minute. Serve hot on a bed of cellophane noodles.

Serves 4
Preparation time: *0 minutes*
Cooking time: *8–10 minutes*

clipboard: The technique of shredding food is often used in stir-frying, so it is useful to learn it. The simplest method is to stack thin slices of food on top of each other. Then, using a cleaver or a sharp knife, cut the food crossways into thin, even strips.

Spring Lamb

stir-fried with garlic and sesame oil

375 g/12 oz lamb fillet
2 tablespoons Chinese wine or dry sherry
2 tablespoons light soy sauce
1 tablespoon dark soy sauce
1 teaspoon sesame oil
2 tablespoons oil
6 garlic cloves, thinly sliced
2.5 cm/1 inch piece root ginger, chopped
1 leek, thinly sliced diagonally
4 spring onions, chopped

cut the lamb into thin slices across the grain.

make the marinade next: mix together the wine or sherry with the soy sauces and sesame oil.

add the lamb and toss to coat. Leave to marinate for 15 minutes.

drain the lamb, reserving the marinade.

heat the oil in a wok or deep frying pan, add the meat and about 2 teaspoons of the marinade and fry briskly for about 2 minutes until the meat is well browned.

add the garlic, ginger, leek and spring onions and fry for a further 3 minutes. Serve at once.

Serves 4
Preparation time: *5 minutes, plus 15 minutes marinating*
Cooking time: *5–7 minutes*

clipboard: Meat is thinly sliced before stir-frying to speed up cooking, and retain maximum tenderness. It should be cut across the grain using a sharp knife or cleaver. If you place the meat in the freezer to harden for about 1 hour before slicing, it will be easy to cut the meat wafer-thin, and it will have defrosted before cooking.

Stir-fried Beef

with white sesame seeds and baby mushrooms

375 g/12 oz rump steak
1 tablespoon light soy sauce
1 tablespoon dark soy sauce
1 tablespoon soft brown sugar
1 teaspoon sesame oil
1 tablespoon Chinese wine or dry sherry
2 tablespoons white sesame seeds
2 tablespoons sunflower oil
1 garlic clove, thinly sliced
2 carrots, sliced diagonally
2 celery sticks, sliced diagonally
50 g/2 oz button mushrooms, sliced

cut the steak into thin slices, slicing across the grain.

combine the soy sauces, sugar, sesame oil and wine or sherry. Toss the meat in this mixture and leave to marinate for 15 minutes.

fry the sesame seeds in a dry pan until they are golden.

heat the oil in a wok or frying pan, add the garlic, celery and carrots and stir-fry briskly for 1 minute.

remove from the wok. Increase the heat, add the beef and stir-fry for about 3 minutes until well browned.

return the vegetables to the wok, add the mushrooms and cook for a further 30 seconds. Sprinkle with the toasted sesame seeds and serve.

Serves 4
Preparation time: *5 minutes, plus 15 minutes marinating*
Cooking time: *6–7 minutes*

clipboard: Sesame seeds are very popular in Chinese cooking because of their nutty flavour and excellent nutritional value. Black and white varieties are available, and taste the same. The white variety are used here to contrast with the colour of the beef.

Stir-fried Beef
in a hot chilli sauce with garlic and ginger

Sizzling hot and full of flavour, this classic stir-fried beef dish will delight lovers of hot, spicy food.

500 g/1 lb rump steak
2 tablespoons sunflower oil
2 dried red chillies
2 garlic cloves, sliced
1 x 2.5 cm/1 inch piece fresh root ginger, shredded
4 spring onions, shredded
2 tablespoons dark soy sauce
2 tablespoons light soy sauce
2 tablespoons Chinese wine or dry sherry
2 fresh green chillies, deseeded and chopped
salt

cut the steak into thin slices across the grain, and season well with salt.

heat the oil in a wok or deep frying pan over a moderate heat and fry the red chillies for 1 minute to flavour the oil.

remove from the wok with a slotted spoon and discard.

increase the heat, then add the pieces of steak and stir-fry for 1minute, until they are browned.

add the garlic, ginger and spring onions and cook for 30 seconds.

pour over the soy sauces and wine or sherry, add the chopped green chillies and cook for a further minute.

transfer to a warmed serving dish and serve at once.

Serves 4
Preparation time: *20minutes*
Cooking time: *4–5 minutes*

Spiced Beef
stir-fried with leeks and celery

*The addition of fresh, crunchy vegetables
to this aromatic stir-fry provides a
satisfying contrast of textures.*

500 g/1 lb rump or sirloin steak
2 medium leeks
3 celery sticks
6 tablespoon oil
1 garlic clove, crushed with a pinch of salt
1 teaspoon red wine vinegar
1 teaspoon soy sauce
1 tablespoon sesame oil
1 tablespoon hot soy bean paste

cut the beef into small, thin slivers. Cut the leeks and celery into matchstick pieces.

heat 3 tablespoons oil in a wok or large frying pan on a high heat.

put in the leeks and celery. Stir-fry for 1 minute and remove.

add the remaining oil to the pan. Put in the steak and stir-fry until it has browned and all the moisture in the pan has evaporated.

stir in the garlic, vinegar, soy sauce, sesame oil and soy bean paste.

add the vegetables and stir-fry for 1 minute.

transfer to a warmed serving dish and serve at once.

Serves 4–6
Preparation time: *10 minutes*
Cooking time: *10 minutes*

Shredded Beef
stir-fried in a hot Szechuan sauce

500 g/1 lb rump or frying steak
2 tablespoons cornflour
3 tablespoons sunflower oil
4 spring onions, chopped
2 celery sticks, sliced diagonally
4 carrots, sliced diagonally
2 tablespoons light soy sauce
1 tablespoon hoisin sauce
3 teaspoons chilli sauce
2 tablespoons Chinese wine or dry sherry
salt

cut the steak across the grain into long, thin, slices.

toss the steak in the cornflour and season with salt to taste.

heat the oil in a wok or frying pan over a moderate heat. Add the spring onions and stir-fry for 1 minute.

add the sliced steak and cook for 4 minutes, stirring, until the meat is lightly browned.

add the celery and carrots and cook for 2 minutes. Stir in the soy, hoisin and chilli sauces, and the wine or sherry.

bring to the boil and cook for 1 minute.

arrange on a warmed serving dish and serve at once.

Serves 4–6
Preparation time: *10–15 minutes*
Cooking time: *about 10 minutes*

clipboard: Hoisin sauce is a thick, brownish-red, soy-based sauce, much used in China both as a condiment and in cooked dishes. It is available in Chinese food stores and large supermarkets.

Steamed Beef
with peppers and Chinese cabbage leaves

500 g/1 lb lean braising steak
25 g/1 oz dried Chinese mushrooms
150 ml/¼ pint boiling Chicken Stock (see page 11)
1 red pepper, cored, deseeded and cut into 2.5cm/1 inch strips
1 green pepper, cored, deseeded and cut into 2.5cm/1 inch strips
1 medium onion, thinly sliced
1 garlic clove, finely chopped
1 teaspoon cornflour
3 tablespoons soy sauce
2 tablespoons sesame oil
1 teaspoon ground ginger
4–6 Chinese cabbage leaves

cut the beef into small, thin slices. Put the mushrooms into a bowl, pour on the stock and leave to soak for 20 minutes.

drain the mushrooms and reserve the stock.

combine the beef, peppers, mushrooms, onion and garlic in a bowl.

mix together the mushroom stock, cornflour, soy sauce, oil and ground ginger and add to the beef.

line the top of a bamboo steamer with the cabbage leaves. Put in the beef mixture. Cover.

bring a small amount of water to the boil in a saucepan. Put in a trivet or stand and set the steamer on top.

cover and steam for 1 hour 15 minutes or until the beef is quite tender. Serve straight from the steamer.

Serves 4–6
Preparation time: *20 minutes, plus 20 minutes soaking*
Cooking time: *1¼–1½ hours*

Stir-fried Beef

with Chinese plum sauce and mushrooms

Plums add a fragrant, fruity sweetness to this mouthwatering beef dish, as well as a succulent contrast of texture.

1 tablespoon sunflower oil

1 onion, thinly sliced

1 garlic clove, crushed

375 g/12 oz lean beef, cut into thin slivers

2–3 dessert plums, pitted and cut into slices

3 flat mushrooms, sliced

1 tablespoon Chinese wine or dry sherry

2 teaspoons soft brown sugar

1 tablespoon dark soy sauce

2 teaspoons cornflour

2 tablespoons water

2 chopped spring onions (green part only), to garnish

heat the oil in a large frying pan, add the onion and fry for 2 minutes. Stir in the garlic and beef and stir-fry over a high heat for 2 minutes.

reduce the heat and add the plums and mushrooms. Continue to stir-fry for 1 minute, then stir in the wine or sherry, sugar and soy sauce.

blend the cornflour with the water to make a thin paste and add this mixture to the pan, stirring until the sauce has thickened.

transfer to a warmed dish and serve at once, garnished with chopped spring onion.

Serves 4
Preparation time: *6 minutes*
Cooking time: *8 minutes*

Stir-fried Kidneys

with spring onions and cauliflower florets

4 lambs' kidneys, halved and cored

2 tablespoons Chinese wine or sherry

I small cauliflower, broken into florets

2 tablespoons oil

4 spring onions, cut into 2.5 cm/1 inch pieces

I tablespoon cornflour

I tablespoon soy sauce

2 tablespoons water

I teaspoon brown sugar

salt

score the kidney halves with shallow criss-cross cuts, about 1 cm/½ inch apart. Marinate in the sherry for 10 minutes.

drain, reserving the marinade. Cook the cauliflower in boiling, salted water for 3 minutes. Drain thoroughly.

heat the oil in a pan. Add the kidneys, spring onions and cauliflower and fry for 2 minutes.

mix the cornflour with the soy sauce, water, sugar, reserved marinade and 1 teaspoon salt.

add to the pan and cook gently for 3 minutes, stirring until the sauce is thickened. Serve hot.

Serves 4
Preparation time: *5 minutes, plus 10 minutes marinating*
Cooking time: *8–10 minutes*

clipboard: Remove any membrane from the kidneys before removing the core. The kidney is scored with criss-cross cuts in order to ensure that maximum tenderness is maintained with speed of cooking.

Stir-fried Liver
with spinach and ginger

The pungent, earthy flavour of spinach blends perfectly with liver in this robust, quickly prepared, stir-fry dish.

375 g/12 oz lamb's liver, cut into thin triangular slices

2 tablespoons cornflour

4 tablespoons sunflower oil

500 g/1 lb fresh spinach, washed and drained

1 teaspoon salt

2 thin slices fresh root ginger, peeled

1 tablespoon light soy sauce

1 tablespoon Chinese wine or dry sherry

spring onion, shredded, to garnish

blanch the slices of liver in boiling water for a few seconds. Drain and coat with cornflour.

heat 2 tablespoons of the oil in a wok or frying pan. Add the spinach and salt and stir-fry for 2 minutes.

remove from the pan and arrange around the edge of a warmed serving dish. Keep hot.

wipe the wok clean with absorbent kitchen paper. Heat the remaining oil in the wok until very hot.

add the ginger, liver, soy sauce and wine or sherry. Stir-fry briskly for 1–2 minutes — avoid overcooking or the liver will become tough.

pour the mixture over the spinach and garnish with spring onions.

Serves 4
Preparation time: *10 minutes*
Cooking time: *4–5 minutes*

clipboard: Blanching liver in boiling water is a good way of ensuring that it remains tender during the cooking process.

Lion's Head Casserole *with garlic*

750 g/1½ lb pork, finely minced
1 teaspoon salt
2 garlic cloves, crushed
1 x 5 cm/2 inch piece fresh root ginger, peeled and chopped
4 tablespoons light soy sauce
3 tablespoons Chinese wine or dry sherry
4 spring onions, chopped
1 tablespoon cornflour
oil for deep frying
300 ml/½ pint Beef Stock (see page 10)
750 g/1½ lb fresh spinach
spring onion, chopped, to garnish (optional)

mix the pork with the salt, garlic, ginger and 1 tablespoon each of the soy sauce and wine or sherry.

add half of the chopped spring onions. Mix in the cornflour and divide the mixture into balls the size of a walnut.

heat the oil in a wok or deep-frier to 160°C/325°F or until a cube of day-old bread browns in 45 seconds.

deep-fry the pork balls until golden. Drain well, then place in a clean pan with the remaining soy sauce, wine or sherry and spring onions.

spoon the stock over, cover and simmer for 15–20 minutes.

wash the spinach leaves and cook in the water clinging to the leaves. When tender, drain well and transfer to a warmed serving dish.

arrange the meatballs on top and garnish with chopped spring onion, if liked. Serve at once.

Serves 4–6
Preparation time: *20 minutes*
Cooking time: *25–30 minutes*

clipboard: This traditional Eastern Chinese dish has its name because the meatballs are said to resemble a lion's head. They are usually served with noodles arranged on top to look like a lion's mane.

Mongolian Hotpot

250 g/8 oz cellophane noodles, or
500 g/1 lb egg noodles
250 g/8 oz lamb. pork or beef fillet, or
a mixture of all 3 meats, thinly sliced
250 g/8 oz boneless chicken breast, skinned
and thinly sliced
250 g/8 oz prawns (whole) or scallops (thinly sliced),
or a mixture of both
250 g/8 oz fish fillets (sole, cod or haddock),
thinly sliced
250 g/8 oz button mushrooms
500 g/1 lb Chinese leaves or Cos lettuce
375 g/12 oz firm bean curd (tofu), cut in small pieces
1.8 litres/3 pints clear stock
1 teaspoon salt
2–3 tablespoons Chinese rice wine or dry sherry

Sauce
4 tablespoons light soy sauce
4 tablespoons dark soy sauce
1 tablespoon sugar
2 teaspoons sesame seed oil
3–4 spring onions, finely shredded
3–4 slices fresh root ginger, peeled and finely
shredded
1–2 garlic cloves, peeled and crushed
1 tablespoon chilli sauce (optional)

soak the noodles in boiling hot water until soft, rinse under cold running water, then drain. Arrange the meats, shellfish, fish, vegetables and bean curd on separate plates or in bowls, then place them on the table.

mix all the ingredients for the sauce together, then divide equally between 4–6 saucers. Place them on the table at individual place settings.

place the hot pot in the centre of the table. Light the charcoal in the funnel and fill the moat with the stock.

add the salt and rice wine or sherry, a little of the Chinese leaves or lettuce, mushrooms, noodles and bean curd. Bring to the boil. Each person picks up a few pieces of meat or fish and swirls them in the stock for a few seconds. When the slices begin to curl and change colour, they should be removed from the liquid and dipped into the sauce before eating.

more vegetables and noodles can be added to the pot from time to time, and eaten with the meat, fish and bean curd. When the meat and fish have been eaten, top up with more stock, add the remaining vegetables and noodles, and recharge with more charcoal if necessary.

bring to the boil and cook for about 1–2 minutes, then ladle the contents into individual bowls. Serve as a soup with the remaining dip sauce, to finish off the meal.

Serves 4–6
Preparation time: *15 minutes*
Cooking time: *about 10 minutes*

clipboard: Inexpensive hot pots or "fire kettles" can be bought at Chinese supermarkets. Alternatively, use an electric wok or rice cooker. Fondues are not suitable, as their burners are not hot enough.

Herbs and vegetables

Dried red chillies

Garlic

Shiitake mushroom

Water chestnut

Dried red chillies

Dried chillies are a relatively recent addition to Chinese cooking, though they are now used extensively, particularly in Szechuan. Chillies are perfect for flavouring oil in stir-frying, and in spicy hot-flavoured pastes and oils. Stored properly they will keep for ages and maintain their red colour and fiery flavour. Use them with care, as they can be searingly hot.

Shiitake mushroom

The shiitake mushroom has a gold/brown cap and light coloured gills and stem. The stems can sometimes be tough and are often discarded, but the caps are intensely fragrant. In China they are often dried, making their flavour even more pronounced. They are one of the key ingredients in Chinese cooking.

Garlic

Garlic is a bulb-shaped, root vegetable, composed of a series of cloves wrapped in a white papery skin. Garlic has been used for thousands of years and has been a major ingredient in the history of cooking. The strong, pungent aroma and flavour adds character to any savoury dish and it is used extensively in Chinese cooking.

Water chestnut

The water chestnut is similar in appearance to the chestnut. A white nut with a brown skin, it is technically the corm of a species of water grass. Water chestnuts have a crunchy texture and sweet taste even when cooked. The Chinese use them extensively in their cooking, both in cooked dishes and in salads. Water chestnuts can be bought fresh or canned.

Bamboo shoot

The bamboo shoot is part of the bamboo plant which is found all over Tropical Asia.

Bamboo shoot

Onion

Coriander

Tofu

Spring onions

It is a pale ivory colour, and the texture varies according to the season. The sweet, crunchy shoots have been used in Chinese cooking since the sixth century, and can be bought fresh or canned.

Tofu

Tofu is a bean curd made from soya beans. It is highly nutritious, and is creamy white in colour with a smooth texture and bland flavour. The curd is pressed and set into cakes. The Chinese use tofu in many ways, in soups, salads and stir-fry dishes. Dried tofu is used as a meat substitute in vegetarian dishes. It is available in supermarkets and Chinese food shops. Fresh tofu should be eaten on the day of purchase.

Onion

The onion has been known and used for thousands of years. The white layered flesh is surrounded by a brown papery skin, and is highly pungent with a sharp flavour. The Chinese use the onion in many of their dishes because its powerful aroma adds great flavour to cooking. It is also used in their pickled dishes.

Spring onions

The spring onion is a long, thin, green onion with a small white bulb. It is sometimes known as a scallion, and has a mild flavour. It can be eaten raw, or used in salads. It is prized in Chinese cooking for its delicate flavour and attractive colour, and also makes an attractive 'tassel' garnish for Chinese dishes.

Coriander

Coriander is otherwise known as Chinese Parsley. It has bright green, lacy leaves and white flowers, and has an intense perfume and flavour. The leaves, roots and seeds are all used in cooking. Coriander is very popular in Chinese, Thai and other oriental styles of cooking. It makes an attractive garnish.

Vegetable dishes

Bean Curd *and sesame salad with peanuts*

375 g/12 oz bean curd (tofu)
125 g/4 oz roast chicken
½ medium cucumber
50 g/2 oz roasted peanuts
oil for deep frying

Dressing

2 tablespoons sesame paste
1 tablespoon soy sauce
1 tablespoon white wine vinegar
1 tablespoon Chinese wine or dry sherry
1 teaspoon chilli sauce
1 garlic clove, crushed with a pinch of salt
2 tablespoons cold water

cut the bean curd, chicken and cucumber into 1 cm/½ inch dice. Put the cucumber, chicken and peanuts into a bowl.

make the dressing: put the sesame paste into a bowl and gradually work in the remaining ingredients to give the consistency of thick mayonnaise.

heat a pan of deep oil to 180°C/350°F or until a cube of day-old bread browns in 45 seconds. Add the cubes of bean curd and deep-fry until they are just turning brown.

remove and drain. Heat the oil to 190°C/375°F. Return the cubes of bean curd to the pan and deep-fry until crisp and golden.

drain the bean curd quickly and mix into the ingredients in the bowl. Mix in the dressing.

serve the salad immediately — if the bean curd is left too long, it will lose its crispness.

Serves 4
Preparation time: *45 minutes*
Cooking time: *8 minutes*

clipboard: Also known as tofu, bean curd is highly nutritious. After cooking the texture is like a honeycomb, so the peanuts add a contrast of crunchy texture. You can make this dish suitable for vegetarians if you like — simply leave out the chicken.

Crispy Bean Curd
with tomato sauce

oil for deep-frying

6 pieces bean curd (tofu), halved then cut into small triangles

3 large tomatoes, skinned, deseeded and finely chopped

150 ml/¼ pint Chicken Stock (see page 11)

1 tablespoon *nam pla*

pinch of salt

⅓ teaspoon sugar

2 spring onion tops, cut into fine strips

heat the oil in a wok or deep fat fryer, add the bean curd and fry until it is golden brown. Remove from the oil with a slotted spoon and set aside.

place the tomatoes in a medium saucepan with the chicken stock, *nam pla*, salt and sugar.

bring to the boil, reduce the heat and simmer for 15–20 minutes.

add the bean curd and simmer for a further 10–15 minutes. The sauce should be thick and tasty.

serve immediately, with strips of spring onion arranged on top.

Serves 4
Preparation time: *15 minutes*
Cooking time *40–45 minutes*

clipboard: The use of tomatoes is unusual in Oriental cookery. This recipe has been influenced by Vietnamese cuisine, which in turn is French influenced. Use a tomato variety that is grown for its flavour. Please note that this recipe uses chicken stock and *nam pla* (a fish product). To make a vegetarian alternative, use vegetable stock and a seaweed-based seasoning (available from health food stores).

Vegetables *in silken tofu and tahini dressing*

This is an elegant dish, made extra healthy and nutritious by the use of tofu in the dressing.

3 dried shiitake mushrooms
½ fennel bulb
2 slices boiled ham
I small carrot, peeled
50 g/2 oz French beans, trimmed
400 ml/14 fl oz Chicken Stock (see page 11)
I tablespoon light soy sauce
2 teaspoons sugar

Dressing
125 g/4 oz silken tofu (bean curd)
2 tablespoons tahini paste
2½ tablespoons sugar
I teaspoon salt

soak the mushrooms in boiling water for 20 minutes. Drain, discard the hard stalks and cut the caps into strips.

cut the fennel, ham, carrot and French beans into diagonal strips.

bring the stock to the boil in a pan with the soy sauce and sugar. Add the vegetables and simmer for 10 minutes. Allow to cool.

make the dressing: drop the tofu into a pan of boiling water, bring back to the boil, then drain.

place on a board, top with a plate and weight to squeeze out excess moisture. Force the tofu through a sieve into a bowl.

add the tahini, sugar and salt. Mix well.

drain the vegetables, reserving the liquid, and add them to the dressing with the ham. Add a little stock to thin if necessary. Serve cold.

Serves 4
Preparation time: *20–30 minutes*
Cooking time: *15–20 minutes*

clipboard: Please note that this recipe uses meat and chicken stock. To make a vegetarian alternative, use vegetable stock and omit the ham.

Braised Chinese Vegetables

2–3 tablespoons dried wood ears or
5–6 Chinese dried mushrooms
250 g/8 oz firm bean curd (tofu)
salt
4 tablespoons vegetable oil
125 g/4 oz carrots, peeled and sliced
125 g/4 oz mangetout, trimmed
125 g/4 oz Chinese leaves, sliced
125 g/4 oz canned, sliced bamboo shoots or
whole baby sweetcorn
1 teaspoon sugar
1 tablespoon light soy sauce
1 teaspoon cornflour
1 tablespoon water
1 teaspoon sesame seed oil, to finish (optional)

soak the wood ears or Chinese dried mushrooms in water to cover for 20–25 minutes; discard the hard roots, then rinse. Cut the mushrooms into small slices.

cut each cake of bean curd into about 12 small pieces, then put them in a saucepan of lightly salted, boiling water for 2–3 minutes, so that they become firm. Remove with a perforated spoon and drain.

heat about half of the oil in a flameproof casserole or heavy-based saucepan until hot. Add the pieces of bean curd and fry until lightly browned on both sides. Remove the bean curd, then heat the remaining oil in the pan.

add the vegetables and stir-fry for about 1–2 minutes. Return the bean curd to the pan, add 1 teaspoon salt, the sugar and soy sauce and stir well. Cover, reduce the heat and braise for 2–3 minutes.

mix the cornflour to a smooth paste with the water. Pour the paste over the vegetables and stir. Increase the heat to high to thicken the sauce, then sprinkle in the sesame seed oil (if using).

Serves 4
Preparation time: *15 minutes, plus 20–25 minutes soaking*
Cooking time: *8–10 minutes*

clipboard: Wood ears, also known as cloud ears, are dried black Chinese fungi with a beautifully delicate flavour. They are available from Chinese grocery stores. Soak them in warm water before use.

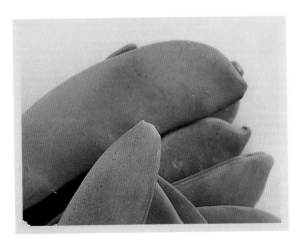

Chinese Leaves
braised with mushrooms

500 g/1 lb Chinese leaves
375 g/12 oz canned straw mushrooms, drained, or
250 g/8 oz fresh button mushrooms
4 tablespoons sunflower oil
2 teaspoons salt
1 teaspoon sugar
1 tablespoon cornflour
3 tablespoons water
50 ml/2 fl oz milk

separate and wash the leaves and cut each one in half lengthways. If using fresh mushrooms, wipe the caps (do not peel) and trim the stalks.

heat 2 tablespoons of the oil in a wok over moderate heat. Add the Chinese leaves and stir-fry for 1 minute.

add 1½ teaspoons of the salt with the sugar and stir-fry for 1 minute. Remove the leaves and arrange neatly on a warmed serving dish. Keep hot.

mix the cornflour to a smooth paste with the water. Heat the remaining oil in the wok until it is hot, add the mushrooms and remaining salt and stir-fry for 1 minute.

add the cornflour paste and the milk and stir constantly until the sauce is smooth, white, and thickened.

pour the sauce evenly over the Chinese leaves and serve at once.

Serves 4
Preparation time: *20 minutes*
Cooking time: *5–10 minutes*

clipboard: Vary this dish by using different mushrooms. Chinese dried mushrooms should be soaked first before using, or, for another really interesting flavour, use shiitake mushrooms.

Festive New Year Pickle

with cucumber, nuts, cauliflower and cabbage

5 cabbage leaves

I cucumber

3 carrots, trimmed

I head cauliflower

1.5 litres/2½ pints vinegar

20 shallots, chopped

2 tablespoons root ginger, shredded

I thumb-size piece fresh turmeric

3 red chillies, deseeded and chopped

2 teaspoons shrimp paste

5 macadamia nuts

I large onion, chopped

6 tablespoons sunflower oil

200 g/7 oz peanuts

3 tablespoons sugar

4 tablespoons sesame seeds

cut the cabbage, cucumber and carrots into narrow strips. Separate the cauliflower into florets.

bring the vinegar to the boil in a saucepan and drop in handfuls of the cabbage, cucumber, carrots, cauliflower and shallots to scald for 1 minute. Lift out and drain well.

work the ginger, turmeric, chillies, shrimp paste, macadamia nuts and onion to a thick paste.

heat the oil in a wok or frying pan and fry this mixture for 5 minutes. Place in a glass or enamel (not metal) bowl and mix in the vegetables thoroughly. Refrigerate for at least 1 day, preferably longer.

to serve, mix in the peanuts and sugar and sprinkle the sesame seeds on top of the pickle.

Serves 4
Preparation time: *45 minutes, plus a day chilling*
Cooking time: *8–10 minutes*

clipboard: The Chinese adore pickles, and this spicy example (called Achar) is prepared in great quantities to celebrate the Chinese New Year.

Crispy Vegetables
deep-fried and served with a spicy avocado dip

Dip

1–2 garlic cloves, chopped
4 tomatoes, peeled, deseeded and chopped
1 teaspoon chilli powder
2 avocado pears, peeled and pitted
1 tablespoon coriander, freshly chopped
pinch of ground coriander (optional)

Batter

125 g/4 oz plain flour
pinch of salt
1 tablespoon sunflower oil
150 ml/¼ pint water
2 egg whites, stiffly whisked

Stir-fry

sunflower oil for deep-frying
500 g/1 lb mixed vegetables, such as cauliflower or
broccoli florets, green beans, whole mushrooms,
mangetout and strips of courgettes

make the dip: place all the ingredients in a blender and blend to a smooth purée. Spoon into a serving dish and chill.

make the batter: sift the flour and salt into a bowl. Gradually beat in the oil and water, then fold in the egg whites.

heat the oil in a wok or frying pan to 180°C/350°F, or until a cube of day-old bread browns in 30 seconds.

dip the vegetables in the batter, then deep-fry them in batches for 2–3 minutes, until they are crisp and golden.

make sure the oil comes back to full heat after each batch.

drain the vegetables on absorbent kitchen paper and serve with the dip.

Serves 6
Preparation time: *15 minutes*
Cooking time: *25–30 minutes*

Spicy Long Beans
with Chinese fish cake

This is a deliciously spicy Chinese recipe for fresh runner beans. Long beans are traditionally used as they are meant to symbolize and ensure a long, happy, life.

8 long French beans or runner beans

I block Chinese fish cake (see clipboard)

3 tablespoons sunflower oil

2 garlic cloves, crushed

I tablespoon chilli bean paste

150 ml/¼ pint water

I teaspoon salt

cut the beans into 5 cm/2 inch lengths, wash and drain.

slice the fish cake into lengths of a similar size.

heat the oil in a wok or frying pan and fry the garlic until light brown.

add the chilli bean paste and cook, stirring all the time, for 1 minute.

add the long beans and cook, stirring well, for 2–3 minutes. Add the fish cake and water.

increase the heat and stir-fry briskly for 1–2 minutes. Add salt to taste and serve immediately.

Serves 4
Preparation time: *10 minutes*
Cooking time: *10–12 minutes*

clipboard: Fishcake is sold in blocks at Chinese supermarkets and can be sliced as required. It is an excellent way of adding flavour and protein to stir-fried vegetables.

Beansprouts and Green Beans
stir-fry with spring onions

500 g/1 lb fresh beansprouts
250 g/8 oz dwarf French beans
3–4 tablespoons sunflower oil
1 spring onion, finely chopped
1 teaspoon salt
1 teaspoon sugar
1 teaspoon sesame oil

wash and rinse the beansprouts in a basin of cold water, discarding the husks and other particles that float to the surface.

drain well. Top, tail and halve the French beans.

heat the oil in a wok until it is smoking. Add the spring onion to flavour the oil, then add the beans and stir a few times.

add the beansprouts and stir-fry for 30 seconds.

add the salt and sugar and stir-fry for 1 minute more.

serve hot, sprinkled with sesame oil.

Serves 4
Preparation time: *10 minutes*
Cooking time: *3–4 minutes*

clipboard: It is best to use fresh beansprouts for this dish, so you should buy them on the day you plan to use them. Canned beansprouts do not have the necessary crunchy texture for use in this recipe.

Mustard-pickled Aubergine

Pickles are very important in Chinese cooking, as they provide a piquant salty or sour contrast to the other foods that are served at a typical meal.

1 medium aubergine, or 6 small long aubergines
750 ml/1¼ pints water
1 tablespoon salt
cucumber rings, to garnish (optional)

Dressing
1 teaspoon mustard powder
3 tablespoons soy sauce
3 tablespoons Chinese wine or medium dry sherry
4 tablespoons sugar

cut the aubergine in 3 mm/⅛ inch slices, and cut each slice into quarters. Soak in the water, with the salt added, for 1 hour.

make the dressing: put all the ingredients in a bowl and stir well.

drain the aubergine slices and pat dry with absorbent kitchen paper.

arrange them carefully in a glass or ceramic serving bowl and pour the dressing over evenly and slowly.

cover the bowl with clingfilm and chill in the refrigerator for several hours or overnight before serving, to allow the flavours to marry.

garnish with the cucumber rings, if liked.

Serves 4
Preparation time: *15 minutes, plus 1 hour soaking and chilling overnight*

clipboard: To make cucumber rings, cut 5mm/¼ inch slices from an unpeeled cucumber and remove the seeds. Make a cut in one ring and loop it through another.

Chinese Cabbage
in sweet and sour sauce

This recipe for Chinese cabbage makes an attractive and different-tasting dish. Children will often enjoy it even if they usually refuse to eat cabbage!

3 tablespoons oil

15 g/½ oz butter

1 Chinese cabbage, cored and shredded

1 teaspoon salt

Sauce

1½ tablespoons cornflour

5 tablespoons water

1½ tablespoons soy sauce

2½ tablespoons sugar

3½ tablespoons vinegar

3½ tablespoons orange juice

2½ tablespoons tomato purée

1½ tablespoons Chinese wine or sherry

heat the oil and butter in a pan. Add the cabbage and sprinkle with the salt. Stir-fry for 2 minutes.

reduce the heat to low and simmer gently for 5–6 minutes.

mix the sauce ingredients in another pan.

bring to the boil and simmer for 4–5 minutes, stirring continuously. until the sauce thickens and becomes translucent.

transfer the cabbage to a serving dish and pour the sauce over it. Serve hot.

Serves 4
Preparation time: *5 minutes*
Cooking time: *11–13 minutes*

clipboard: Chinese cabbage, also called Bok Choy is widely available at greengrocers and supermarkets. It has a crisp, juicy texture, and mild mustard flavour. Swiss chard can be substituted.

Pickled Green Salad *with Chinese cabbage and cucumber*

This is a cool, refreshing and delicately pretty pickled salad, which is much enjoyed in Chinese cooking as a contrast with hot, fiery dishes.

500 g/1 lb cucumber, peeled
500 g/1 lb Chinese cabbage, cored and chopped
2 teaspoons salt
1 teaspoon garlic, crushed
1 teaspoon Szechuan or black peppercorns, ground
1 teaspoon sugar
1 tablespoon light soy sauce
2 tablespoons sesame oil
1 tablespoon red wine vinegar

crush the cucumber until cracks appear on the surface. Quarter it lengthways, then cut into pieces.

put in a bowl with the cabbage, sprinkle with salt and leave for 2 hours.

rinse the salt from the vegetables and drain on absorbent kitchen paper. Mix together the garlic, pepper, sugar, soy sauce, oil and vinegar.

pour over the vegetables, mix well and allow to stand for at least 3 hours before serving.

Serves 4–6
Preparation time: *15 minutes, plus 3 hours standing*

clipboard: Szechuan peppercorns are not related to ordinary pepper. They are reddish brown, and are far more aromatic and pungent than ordinary peppercorns. The cucumber in this recipe is salted in order to extract its indigestible juices and to ensure as crisp a texture as possible.

Fruit and vegetables

Bok Choy

Chinese leaves

Aubergine

Baby corn

Bok Choy

Bok choy is sometimes called Chinese chard or Chinese white cabbage. Now widely available in grocers and supermarkets, as well as from Chinese food shops, it has thick white stems and dark green leaves. Bok Choy is mild in flavour and can be eaten raw or braised. There is a smaller variety known as a baby bok choy. Braised whole, this is a popular vegetable dish served at special banquets.

Aubergine

The aubergine is sometimes known as eggplant, because of its shape, though there is a wide variation in its size, colour, flavour and shape. All are characterized by a smooth, purple skin and pale green/cream flesh. It is technically a fruit but is usually cooked and eaten as a vegetable. It originates from south-east Asia, and can be steamed, boiled, grilled, or sautéed. The baby aubergine is a miniature version, and is prized for its tender, sweet flesh. It is a very popular ingredient in Chinese cooking, especially in traditional winter pickles.

Chinese leaves

Chinese leaves are pale green leaves which grow tightly packed to form a long, slim, tapering cabbage. It has a clean, delicate flavour and can be used in salads, stir-fries or as a steamed vegetable. It is also frequently used in Chinese soups. Originating in Eastern Asia several hundred years ago, it is best eaten from early autumn to winter, but is now imported all year round.

Baby corn

Baby corn is a delicious, finger-sized corn which is pale yellow in colour, with a delicate, sweet flavour. It is a miniature version of corn on the cob or sweet corn. Baby corn is ideal as an ingredient in stir-fry dishes

Lychees

Pineapple

Lemon

Plum

and can also be plain boiled as a separate vegetable accompaniment. It is easily available in the summer and autumn months.

Plum

The plum is a small oval-shaped fruit with a shiny skin, ranging in colour from yellow to purple. It has sweet, juicy flesh with a single stone. It is delicious eaten by itself and is used in Chinese cooking for both savoury and sweet dishes. A delicious plum sauce is made from the fruit, and this is often served with duck. Plums are at their best in summer and early autumn.

Lychees

The lychee is a small, oval cherry-sized fruit with a pretty pink or red outer casing which is covered with tiny bumps. The translucent white flesh encases a single stone. The fruit of an evergreen tree from south-east China, the lychee has a delicious grape-like flavour. Lychees are often used in fruit salad or in savoury dishes. They are at their best in summer, but are available canned all year round.

Pineapple

Pineapple is a tropical fruit with a thick yellow/brown skin and a cactus-like crown. The yellow flesh is sweet and juicy and is delicious eaten by itself or added to savoury or sweet dishes. Peak season for pineapple is spring but it is also available canned. It is named because of its resemblance to a pine cone.

Lemon

The lemon is an oval citrus fruit with tart-tasting flesh. It is mainly used as an addition to dishes rather than being eaten by itself, and the juice and fragrant rind are used in both sweet and savoury dishes.
The lemon is a good source of vitamin C and it is widely available all year round.

Desserts

Toffee Apples
Peking-style

These scrumptious apple pieces, encased in crisp, fine, toffee jackets, make a popular dessert, served in Chinese restaurants all over the world.

125 g/4 oz plain flour
I egg
100 ml/3½ fl oz water, plus 2 tablespoons
4 crisp apples, peeled, cored and cut into thick slices
600 ml/I pint sunflower oil, plus I tablespoon
6 tablespoons sugar
3 tablespoons golden syrup

mix together the flour, egg and 100 ml/3½ fl oz of the water to make a batter. Dip each piece of apple into the batter.

heat 600 ml/1 pint of the oil in a wok or deep frying pan to 180°C/350°F or until a cube of bread browns in 30 seconds.

deep-fry the apple pieces for 2 minutes, then remove and drain on absorbent kitchen towels.

heat together the sugar in another pan, and add the remaining oil and water. Dissolve the sugar over a gentle heat, then simmer for 5 minutes, stirring constantly.

add the golden syrup and boil until the hard crack stage is reached, at 151°C/304°F, or until it forms brittle threads when dropped into iced water. Put in the fried apples and turn to coat each piece.

remove the apple pieces with a slotted spoon and drop into iced water.

Serves 4
Preparation time: *15 minutes*
Cooking time: *about 16 minutes*

Banana Fritters
deep-fried in batter

The addition of lime as a flavouring for this traditional Chinese dessert provides an unusual and refreshing touch.

125 g/4 oz self-raising flour
40 g/1½ oz rice flour
½ teaspoon salt
rind of 1 lime, finely grated (optional)
vegetable oil, for deep-frying
8 small bananas

To serve
12 limes, cut into quarters
caster sugar, to taste

sift the flours and salt into a bowl. Add about 200 ml/7 fl oz cold water and whisk thoroughly to make a smooth, coating batter.

stir in the grated lime rind (if using).

heat the oil in a hot wok or deep-fat fryer. Meanwhile, peel the bananas, spear them one at a time with a skewer and dip into the batter until they are evenly coated.

deep-fry the bananas in batches until they are crisp and golden. Remove with a perforated spoon. Drain on absorbent kitchen paper.

serve hot, with the lime wedges and sugar for sprinkling.

Serves 8
Preparation time: *15 minutes*
Cooking time: *12–16 minutes*

clipboard: If possible, buy very small bananas for these fritters. They look better than large ones and are usually sweeter in flavour. You are most likely to find them in Asian grocery stores.

Fried Sweet Potato Balls

with candied fruits and sesame seeds

Created from sweet potatoes, an unusual dessert ingredient, these are absolutely delicious!

500 g/1 lb sweet potatoes
125 g/4 oz rice flour
50 g/2 oz soft brown sugar
125 g/4 oz crystallized fruit, chopped
50 g/2 oz sesame seeds, lightly toasted
oil for deep-frying

cook the potatoes in boiling water for 20 minutes until tender; drain and remove the peel.

mash the flesh and gradually beat in the flour and sugar. Stir in the crystallized fruit.

roll the mixture into walnut-sized balls with dampened hands, then coat with sesame seeds.

heat the oil in a wok or deep-fryer and deep-fry the potato balls for 5–7 minutes, until golden brown. Drain on absorbent kitchen paper. Serve hot.

Serves 4–6
Preparation time: *10 minutes*
Cooking time: *25–27 minutes*

clipboard: Sesame seeds are often toasted before using, in order to bring out their deliciously nutty flavour. To do this easily, simply dry-fry them in the wok for 2–3 minutes, or until they are golden brown.

Rice Fritters
with coconut and vanilla

These delectable tit-bits simply melt in the mouth — they are crispy outside and softly succulent within.

165 g/5½ oz medium grain rice, cooked (see page 132)
2 eggs, beaten
3 tablespoons sugar
½ teaspoon vanilla essence
50 g/2 oz plain flour
1 tablespoon baking powder
pinch of salt
25 g/1 oz desiccated coconut
vegetable oil for deep-frying
sifted icing sugar, for sprinkling

put the rice, eggs, sugar and vanilla in a bowl, and mix well.

sift together the flour, baking powder and salt, then stir into the rice mixture. Stir in the coconut.

heat the oil in a deep fat fryer to 180°C/350°F or until a cube of day-old bread browns in 30 seconds.

drop tablespoonfuls of the mixture into the hot oil, one at a time, and deep-fry until golden on all sides. Drain on absorbent kitchen paper.

transfer to a warmed serving dish and sprinkle with a generous amount of icing sugar. Serve hot.

Makes about 20
Preparation time: *10 minutes*
Cooking time: *about 8–10 minutes*

clipboard: As rice is such a staple food in China, it is not surprising that so many desserts are based on sweetened rice. Many of these are essential fare at the festive meals that punctuate the year.

Plum Blossom and Snow

The fruit symbolizes the first blossom of spring, and the white topping is the snow left over after winter.

6 eating apples
6 bananas
2 lemons
6 eggs, separated
375 g/12 oz sugar
9 tablespoons milk
9 tablespoons cornflour
rind of 1 lime, thinly pared, to decorate

peel and core the apples and slice thinly. Peel the bananas and slice thinly. With a potato peeler, thinly pare the rind of 1 lemon and set aside for the decoration. Squeeze the juice from both lemons. Arrange the apple and banana in alternate layers in 12 individual ovenproof dishes, sprinkling each layer with a little of the lemon juice.

put the egg yolks in a heavy-based saucepan with the sugar, milk, cornflour and 140 ml/4½ fl oz cold water. Stir well to mix, then heat very gently, stirring all the time, until smooth.

pour the custard mixture over the fruit. Beat the egg whites until stiff, then spread over the top. Bake in a preheated hot oven at 220°C/425°F, Gas Mark 7 for 5 minutes, or until the top is crisp and golden. Remove the dishes from the oven and leave until completely cold.

meanwhile, prepare the decoration. Plunge the pared lemon and lime rind into a saucepan of boiling water and blanch for 2 minutes. Drain; refresh under cold running water, then pat dry with absorbent kitchen paper and cut into thin strips. Sprinkle evenly over the top of the cold desserts just before serving.

Serves 12
Preparation time: *30 minutes*
Cooking time: *about 5 minutes*
Oven temperature: *220°C/425°F/Gas Mark 7*

Almond Float

with mixed fruits

Cool and delicately flavoured, this almond-scented float provides a light, clean-tasting finish to a meal.

15 g/½ oz agar-agar or isinglass, or 25 g/1 oz powdered gelatine
4 tablespoons sugar
300 ml/½ pint milk
1 teaspoon almond flavouring
1 x 425 g/14 oz can apricots, or mixed fruit salad
50 g/2 oz white grapes, peeled and deseeded

dissolve the agar-agar or isinglass in 300 ml/½ pint water over a gentle heat. (If you are using gelatine, dissolve it in the water according to the packet instructions.)

dissolve the sugar in 300 ml/½ pint water in a separate saucepan, then combine with the dissolved setting agent and add the milk and almond flavouring. Pour this mixture into a large serving bowl.

leave until cold, then chill in the refrigerator for at least 3 hours, until it is completely set.

to serve, cut into small cubes and place in a serving bowl. Add the canned fruit and syrup, then add the grapes and mix well. Serve chilled.

Serves 4
Preparation time: *20 minutes, plus 3 hours setting*
Cooking time: *20 minutes*

clipboard: Agar-agar is an extremely useful setting agent which has no flavour of its own, and does not require refrigeration.

Almond Biscuits

These fragrant biscuits are not a typical dessert, they are more of an end-of-meal snack to clear the palate. They are very popular with the family, so make plenty, and keep them in an airtight storage jar.

175 g/6 oz flour
pinch of salt
½ teaspoon bicarbonate of soda
75 g/3 oz lard
25 g/1 oz ground almonds
75 g/3 oz sugar
1 egg
½ teaspoon almond essence
15 blanched almonds
1 egg yolk, beaten with 1 tablespoon water

sift the flour with the salt and bicarbonate of soda.

rub in the lard, mix in the ground almonds and sugar. Bind the mixture with the egg and almond essence and knead into a pliable dough.

make the dough into 15 small balls. Lay on a floured baking sheet and flatten to a thickness of 5 mm/¼ inch.

press a blanched almond into the centre of each biscuit and brush with the egg and water mixture.

bake the biscuits in a preheated oven at 180°C/350°F/Gas Mark 4 for 15 minutes, or until they are light brown.

lift on to a wire rack to cool.

Makes 15 biscuits
Preparation time: *15 minutes*
Cooking time: *15 minutes*
Oven temperature: *180°C/350°F/Gas Mark 4*

Lychee Sorbet

Make this luscious sorbet when you want a cool, refreshing and pretty finish to a meal.

1 x 500 g/1 lb can lychees
125 g/4 oz granulated sugar
2 tablespoons lemon or lime juice
2 egg whites
rind of 1 lime, thinly pared, to decorate

drain the juice from the lychees into a measuring jug and make up to 300 ml/½ pint with cold water. Pour into a saucepan and stir in the sugar. Heat gently until the sugar has dissolved, then bring to the boil. Simmer gently, without stirring, for 10 minutes, then remove from the heat. Set aside and allow to cool slightly.

purée the lychees in a blender or food processor or press through a sieve, then mix with the sugar syrup and lemon or lime juice. Pour the mixture into a shallow freezer container and place in the freezer for 1–2 hours, or until nearly frozen.

whisk the egg whites in a clean, dry bowl until fairly stiff. Cut the frozen mixture into small pieces, then work in a blender or food processor to break down the crystals. Without allowing the mixture to melt, quickly fold in the whisked egg white until evenly incorporated, then pour into a slightly deeper freezer container. Return to the freezer for 2–3 hours or until firm.

meanwhile, prepare the decoration. Plunge the lime rind into a saucepan of boiling water and blanch for 2 minutes. Drain, refresh under cold running water, then pat dry with absorbent kitchen paper and cut into thin strips.

to serve the sorbet, remove from the freezer 10 minutes before serving. Scoop the sorbet into individual glass dishes and sprinkle with the lime rind. Serve immediately.

Serves 6
Preparation time: *30 minutes, plus 3–5 hours freezing*
Cooking time: *10 minutes*

Dim sum

Pork dim sum

King Prawn
Dumpling

Pork and shark fin dumpling

Steamed dumpling

Pork dim sum

The term 'dim sum' encompasses a wide range of little snacks and light meals popular throughout China. They have been served for generations in Chinese tea houses, and can also be made at home. A literal translation of dim sum means 'touch the heart' which indicates the affection with which these delicious titbits and savoury morsels are regarded. The custom is to sample many kinds of different tastes and textures in tiny portions. At the same time, vast quantities of steaming hot tea are consumed — this is really necessary, because some dim sum can be very rich, and the tea aids digestion. In Chinese communities, whole families gather on Sunday mornings and enjoy their gossip and *yum cha*, which means 'drink tea'. Dim sum are served as a speciality on the menu of many Chinese restaurants. A wide selection is brought to the table in a special trolley with heated compartments. The guests choose their favourites from the trolley selection, which is frequently replenished.

Pork and shark fin dumpling

This dumpling is deep-fried and contains morsels of pork and shark's fin. Shark's fins are much sought after in China, and as a consequence are very expensive. They are famous for their alleged aphrodisiac properties. The best shark's fins are found in China and the Philippines. The fins are soaked overnight and then boiled for three hours to prepare this delicacy.

King Prawn Dumpling

This dumpling is fragrant, pretty and tastes utterly delicious! It has a translucent wrapper which surrounds a pale pink filling of king prawns, fresh ginger, water chestnut and

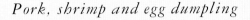

Pork, shrimp and egg dumpling

Char Sui Bao

Wonton

coriander. The dumpling is steamed over a bamboo steamer and is usually served with soy sauce or chilli oil for dipping.

Steamed pork dumpling
Steamed dumplings are very popular in China. To make the filling, minced pork is combined with soy sauce, ginger and Chinese wine.

The filling is then placed in flat dough circles, which are gathered up into a parcel and steamed. They should be served hot with sweet and sour sauce.

Char Sui Bao
A char sui bao is a steamed pork bun and is one of the most popular of the dim sum selection. The filling consists of barbecued pork, red bean curd, soy sauce, onion, ginger and garlic. This filling is placed in the middle of the special bread dough and the buns are then steamed until cooked.

Pork, shrimp and egg dumpling
The pork, shrimp and egg mixture is placed in the centre of a round noodle wrapper, which is then gathered up to make a nest with an open top. The dumpling is then deep fried, and served hot with a chilli or soy sauce dip.

Wonton
The Wonton is probably the best known of the dim sum selection. To make them, you need wonton skins, which are rather fiddly to make at home, especially if you are inexperienced. This need not deter you from making your own wonton, as ready-made skins are available at Chinese food stores. The skin is folded over a small amount of stuffing. This consists of ground pork with seasoning. These are then deep-fried until they are crisp and golden. Wonton are served with sweet and sour sauce.

Breads and Pancakes

Pancake Rolls
with chicken and mushrooms

Pancake batter
250 g/8 oz plain flour

pinch of salt

1 egg

about 300 ml/½ pint water

Filling
1 tablespoon oil

1 teaspoon root ginger, chopped

2 garlic cloves, crushed

250 g/8 oz chicken breast, skinned and diced

2 tablespoons soy sauce

1 tablespoon Chinese wine or dry sherry

125 g/4 oz mushrooms, sliced

3 spring onions, chopped

50 g/2 oz peeled prawns

sift the flour and salt into a bowl, add the egg and beat in sufficient water to make a smooth batter.

lightly oil a 20 cm/8 inch frying pan and place over moderate heat. When the pan is very hot, pour in just enough batter to cover the bottom thinly, tilting the pan to spread it evenly. Cook the pancake for 30 seconds or until the underside is just firm, then carefully remove from the pan. Repeat with the remaining batter — it should make about 12 pancakes. Keep the pancakes warm while making the filling.

make the filling: heat the oil in a wok or frying pan, add the ginger and garlic and fry for 30 seconds. Add the chicken and brown quickly.

stir in the soy sauce and wine or sherry, then the mushrooms and spring onions. Increase the heat and cook for 1 minute.

remove from the heat, stir in the prawns and cool.

place 2–3 tablespoons of the filling in the centre of each pancake. Fold in the sides and form into a tight roll, sealing the edge with a little flour and water paste.

deep-fry the rolls a few at a time for 2–3 minutes. Drain on absorbent kitchen paper, then serve hot with soy sauce as a dip, if liked.

Serves 4–6
Preparation time: *10 minutes*
Cooking time: *45 minutes*

clipboard: The chicken in this recipe could be replaced with shredded cooked pork, beef or turkey.

Stuffed Pancakes
filled with sweet bean paste

Pancake batter

250 g/8 oz plain flour
1 egg, beaten
300 ml/½ pint water

Filling

6–8 tablespoons sweet red bean paste
or dates, finely chopped
vegetable oil for deep-frying

put the flour into a large bowl, make a well in the centre and add the egg. Add the water gradually, beating constantly, to make a smooth batter.

lightly oil an 18 cm/7 inch frying pan and place over moderate heat. When the pan is very hot, pour in just enough batter to cover the bottom thinly, tilting the pan to spread it evenly.

cook for 30 seconds or until the underside is just firm, then carefully remove from the pan. Repeat with the remaining batter — it should make about 12 pancakes.

divide the sweet red bean paste or dates equally between the pancakes, placing it in the centre of the uncooked side of each one.

fold the bottom edge over the filling, then fold the sides towards the centre, to form an envelope. Brush the edge of the top flap with a little water, fold down and press the edges together firmly to seal.

heat the oil in a deep-fat fryer and fry the pancakes for 1 minute or until crisp and golden. Remove and drain on absorbent kitchen paper. Cut each pancake into 6 or 8 slices. Serve hot, with Chinese tea.

Serves 4–6
Preparation time: *20 minutes*
Cooking time: *15–20 minutes*

clipboard: Sweet bean paste is a thick soya bean paste sold in cans in Chinese food stores. It is often used as a base for sweet sauces.

Mandarin Pancakes

These are the traditional pancakes served with Peking Duck.

500 g/1 lb flour
300 ml/½ pint boiling water
1 tablespoon oil
3 tablespoons sesame oil

sift the flour into a mixing bowl and make a well in the centre. Mix together the water and oil and gradually stir into the flour using chopsticks or a wooden spoon. Turn the dough on to a floured work top and knead until firm. Let the dough rest for 10 minutes.

divide the dough into 3 and roll each piece into a sausage shape about 5 cm/2 inches in diameter. Cut each one into 8. Roll the small pieces to thin, flat pancakes about 18 cm/7 inches in diameter. Brush one side of half the pancakes with sesame oil. Sandwich them together with the remaining pancakes.

set a heavy frying pan on a high heat without any fat. When the pan is hot, reduce the heat to moderate. Fry one pancake sandwich at a time, turning it over when it starts to rise and bubble and when small brown spots appear on the underside.

when both sides are done, gently peel the 2 pancakes apart and fold each one in half, oiled side inwards. Cook the remaining pancakes in the same way, keeping them warm in a low oven as the rest are cooked.

Makes 24 pancakes
Preparation time: *20 minutes, plus 10 minutes resting*
Cooking time: *about 15–20 minutes*

clipboard: The recipe for Peking Duck is on page 92. These pancakes can be made in advance, wrapped in a clean linen tea cloth and reheated in a low oven when needed.

Spring Rolls
with chicken and crab

Filling

50 g/2 oz cellophane noodles, soaked in water for
10 minutes and cut into 2.5 cm/1 inch pieces
500 g/1 lb chicken breast meat, cut into thin strips
2 tablespoons dried wood ears (see page 192)
soaked in warm water for 20 minutes
and finely chopped
3 garlic cloves, finely chopped
3 shallots, finely chopped
250 g/8 oz crabmeat
sunflower oil for deep-frying
pepper

For the wrappers
4 eggs, beaten
20 spring roll wrappers

To garnish
spring onion tassels, to
garnish (see page 62)

make the filling: put the ingredients in a bowl and mix well. Divide into 20 portions and shape into small cylinder shapes.

brush beaten egg over the entire surface of each spring roll wrapper. Leave for a few minutes until soft.

place the filling along the curved edge of the spring roll wrapper, roll once, then fold over the sides to enclose and continue rolling.

heat the oil until a cube of day-old bread browns in 30 seconds. Fry the spring rolls, 5 or 6 at a time, until golden all over.

drain well on absorbent kitchen paper. Serve hot or warm, garnished with spring onion tassels.

Makes 20
Preparation time: *30 minutes*
Cooking time: *about 10 minutes*

clipboard: Spring roll wrappers are specially designed for the purpose and are sold in Chinese food stores. If you are unable to obtain them, use frozen filo pastry instead, cut into squares. Defrost the pastry and use it according to the packet instructions.

Prawn Toasts
with ham and sesame seeds

These crunchy toasts have a superb flavour — they are a delicious snack in their own right, or can be served as part of a Chinese meal.

I teaspoon Chinese wine or dry sherry
I teaspoon salt
I egg white
I teaspoon cornflour
500 g/I lb prawns, shelled, deveined and finely chopped
7 slices of white bread from a large sliced loaf, with the crusts removed
2 tablespoons sesame seeds
2 tablespoons cooked ham, chopped
oil for deep frying
parsley sprigs, to garnish

place the wine or sherry, salt, egg white and cornflour in a bowl and mix until smooth. Stir in the prawns.

divide this mixture between the bread slices.

sprinkle with the sesame seeds and ham and press the topping firmly into the bread, using the back of a spoon.

heat the oil to 180°C/350°F or until a cube of day-old bread browns in 30 seconds. Deep-fry the toasts, a few at a time, with the prawn side facing down.

when the edges of the bread turn golden, turn to the other side. Fry until golden brown.

drain on absorbent kitchen paper and cut each slice of bread into 4 squares. Arrange on a serving plate, garnish with parsley and serve hot.

Makes 28
Preparation time: *20 minutes*
Cooking time: *20–25 minutes*

Crab Fritters
with water chestnuts

These little fritters are ideal to serve as a party snack with drinks, as well as making a savoury addition to a complete meal.

375 g/12 oz crab meat, finely chopped
50 g/2 oz pork fat, minced
4 water chestnuts, peeled and finely chopped
1 egg white
2 tablespoons cornflour
1 tablespoon Chinese wine or dry sherry
sunflower oil for deep-frying
salt and pepper

place the crab meat in a bowl with the pork fat and water chestnuts and blend well.

add the egg white, cornflour, salt and pepper and wine or sherry and mix together.

heat the oil in a wok or pan to 180°C/350°F or until a cube of day-old bread browns in 30 seconds.

using a teaspoon, scoop up 1 spoonful of the crab mixture at a time and lower it into the hot oil.

fry the balls until they are golden brown, remove with a slotted spoon and drain on absorbent kitchen paper.

they should be crisp on the outside and tender inside. Serve hot.

Serves 4
Preparation time: *about 30 minutes*
Cooking time: *15–20 minutes*

clipboard: Deep-frying is a popular Chinese cooking technique, used here to cook these fritters.

Dumplings
with pork and shrimps

Dough

500 g/1 lb plain flour
175 ml/6 fl oz boiling water
125 ml/4 fl oz cold water

Filling

500 g/1 lb pork, minced
500 g/1 lb shrimps, peeled and minced
125 g/4 oz spring onion, finely chopped
1 tablespoon root ginger, shredded
1 tablespoon light soy sauce
1½ teaspoons salt
freshly ground black pepper
1 bunch watercress, coarsely chopped
5½ tablespoons sunflower oil

Dip

2 tablespoons wine vinegar
2 tablespoons soy sauce

make the dough: place the flour in a bowl with the boiling water. Beat well until smooth. Leave to rest for 2–3 minutes. Add the cold water and knead well.

make the filling: mix together the pork, shrimps, spring onion, ginger, soy sauce, salt and pepper. Add the chopped watercress and 1 tablespoon of the oil. Blend well together.

roll the dough into a long sausage shape 4 cm/1½ inch lengths. Roll each one flat to make small pancake shapes. Place 1 tablespoon of stuffing on each pancake then fold in half. Pinch the edges together to close firmly.

heat a wok and place 3 tablespoons of oil in it. Tilt the wok several times until the surface is evenly oiled. Arrange the dumplings evenly over the surface of the pan. Turn the heat to high and shallow-fry for 2–3 minutes to brown the underside of the dumplings.

add 120 ml/4 fl oz water to the wok and cover. Steam the dumplings over high heat until almost all the water has evaporated. Remove the cover and pour in 1½ tablespoons of hot oil from the side. Reduce the heat and cook until all the liquid has evaporated.

mix the wine vinegar and soy sauce together to make a dipping sauce.

Serves 4–6
Preparation time: *20 minutes, plus 2–3 minutes resting*
Cooking time: *10-12 minutes*

Meat Dumplings
with pork and ginger

Dough
500 g/1 lb plain flour
4 teaspoons baking powder
250 ml/8 fl oz water

Filling
500 g/1 lb pork, minced
1 tablespoon Chinese wine or dry sherry
3 tablespoons light soy sauce
2 teaspoons sugar
1 teaspoon salt
1 tablespoon sesame oil
2 teaspoons fresh ginger root, finely chopped
1 teaspoon cornflour

sift together the flour and baking powder into a bowl. Add the water and knead well.

cover with a damp cloth and place a small plate on top. Leave the dough to rise for 2 hours.

combine the pork with the wine or sherry, soy sauce, sugar, salt, sesame oil, ginger and cornflour.

divide the dough in half. Knead lightly and roll each half into a sausage shape 5 cm/2 inches in diameter.

divide each into about 15 rounds. Flatten the rounds, then roll out to make circles 7.5 cm/3 inches in diameter.

place a tablespoon of filling on each circle. Gather up the sides of the dough to meet at the top, and twist to seal tightly.

arrange the dumplings 1 cm/½ inch apart on a piece of damp muslin in a steamer. Cover and steam vigorously for 20 minutes.

drain if necessary and serve hot.

Serves 4
Preparation time: *30 minutes, plus 2 hours rising*
Cooking time: *20 minutes*

Crispy Wonton
with sweet and sour sauce

500 g/1 lb wonton skins
3 tablespoons light soy sauce
1 tablespoon Chinese wine or dry sherry
500 g/1 lb lean pork, minced
1 teaspoon brown sugar
1 garlic clove, crushed
1 x 2.5 cm/1 inch piece fresh root ginger,
peeled and finely chopped
250 g/8 oz frozen leaf spinach, thawed
sunflower oil for deep-frying

Sauce
2 garlic cloves, crushed
1 tablespoon sunflower oil
2 tablespoons light soy sauce
2 tablespoons clear honey
2 tablespoons wine vinegar
2 tablespoons tomato purée
2 teaspoons chilli sauce
2 tablespoons Chinese wine
2 teaspoons of a thin cornflour and water paste

cut out 5 cm/2 inch squares from the wonton skins. Put the soy sauce, sherry and pork in a bowl and mix well.

add the sugar, garlic and ginger. Squeeze excess liquid from the spinach in a clean cloth and add to the mixture. Combine well.

spoon 1 tablespoon of the mixture on to the centre of each wonton. Dampen the edges and fold to form triangles, pressing the edges together firmly so that the filling does not come out during frying.

heat the oil to 180°C/350°F or until a cube of day-old bread browns in 30 seconds.

fry the wonton, a few at a time, for about 5 minutes until golden. Drain on absorbent kitchen paper.

make the sauce: stir-fry the garlic in the sunflower oil. Add all of the other ingredients. Bring to the boil, and cook for 2 minutes. Serve the wonton hot with the sweet and sour sauce.

Serves 4–6
Preparation time: *20 minutes*
Cooking time: *about 20 minutes*

clipboard: Wonton skins are made from a thin yellow dough, ready-packed in cellophane. You can buy them from Chinese food stores. Wonton are usually served as part of an assortment of dim sum, or teatime snacks, in Chinese teahouses.

Index

Acknowledgments

Photo Credits
Jean Cazals: front cover, back cover

Special photography by Jean Cazals

All other photos:
Octopus Publishing Group Ltd. / William Adams-Lingwood, Bryce Attwell, Robert Golden, Melvyn Grey, Christine Hanscomb, Tim Imrie, David Johnson, Paul Kemp, Graham Kirk, Vernon Morgan, James Murphy, Peter Myers, Ian O'Leary, Paul Williams.

Home economist
Marie-Ange Lapierre